RV CAMPING COMPLETE GUIDE

[8 IN 1] THE COMPLETE GUIDE WITH EVERYTHING YOU NEED TO KNOW ON HOW TO MAKE LIFE ON THE ROAD EASIER, WITH OVER 2500 CAMPGROUNDS & ATTRACTIONS TO VISIT IN THE 50 STATES

D1518889

BY ADAM STEPHENS

☐ Table of Contents

⬜   Introduction

There are many questions you could ask as a new camper. Below is an actual list of frequently asked questions that every camp beginner will ask. I recommend not going camping until you have answered all of your questions and understand the requirements that are expected of you.

Camping descriptions:

Camping in RV (or camping with a recreational vehicle) is like living at home because you bring a furnished vehicle in which you live.

Where to camp?

They all offer more or less the same facilities, such as bathrooms, hot water for showers and commercial areas; They are handy for beginners. Camping in such places is not very expensive. They can charge between $ 10 and $25 per night.

Private camps may or may not offer the amenities, and may cost more. Also, they are only allowed to allow a certain number of campers on their site.

However, you need to make sure you know if this is allowed in the area you selected. In that case, remember that there are no services like a laundromat, restrooms, or a camp store nearby.

What camping gear should I wear?

The answer to this specific question depends on where you are camping. You can buy all the camping gear at the sports store or Walmart. Don't buy expensive equipment because you have no experience caring for it.

If you are camping in free camps, you will likely get a grill or barbecue and all the cooking ingredients from the actual camp store. Apart from that, you must bring the other essential items such as clothes, tents, bags and pads, kitchen supplies like charcoal and spatula, kettle, cups, plates, spoons, and a pot or two. You can actually buy all the camping gear at the sports store or Walmart. Don't buy expensive equipment because you have no experience caring for it.

If you are camping in free camps, you will likely get a grill or barbecue and all the actual cooking ingredients from the camp store. Apart from that, you should bring other essentials such as clothes, tents, sleeping bags, from home.

What clothes should I wear when camping?

Be sure to wear full sleeves when camping.

There are many things to actually consider when setting up your camp. Launching tents in a high place is essential, but be sure not to choose a field on a slope. It is better to select a location near a water source, such as a fountain, to avoid wasting time getting water. Beginner or not, you should have the following items with you on a camping trip. Make sure your camping trip checklist includes all of the following.

- ☐ The flashlight is a must. Always use it.

- ☐ Matchbox to light the stove and for the campfire.

- ☐ Water should be abundant, so you don't run out of the water while camping.

- ☐ Sweater and some waterproof clothing for added protection.

- ☐ Machete to help you cut the bushes while you go to your camp or go for a walk.

- ☐ The Swiss knife is always useful.

Good walking shoes should never be forgotten, and you walk on uneven terrain with lots of greenery and small animals around you.

Biodegradable soap is preferable to other solvents because it is more environmentally friendly.

Use cheaper but good quality until you learn how to use a tent.

When lighting the fire, be careful not to burn it too close to the tent, as the flap of the canvas can catch fire in strong winds.

While throwing garbage, be sure to throw it in the bins and not around the camp.

Use biodegradable soap while washing utensils or yourself, as it is eco-friendly.

Plan meals before going for a walk. You may be late and hungry. Also, bring enough to last until the end of your trip.

Get used to the camping gear when you first buy it. It is ideal for overnight camping in your backyard for a cramping feeling.

Camp close to home for your first camping trip so you can get home faster if you don't like the experience.

There are several benefits of camping, such as being closer, not having a television to enter family time, and a walk-in nature.

Chapter 1.   What is an RV?

One of the actual most important things to actually know about RV living is that the term "RV" is a specific type of vehicle. If you are considering RV living, you have to understand what an RV is and your different options. In short, an RV is a recreational vehicle. Motorhomes, trailers, and truck campers count as RVs because they have living quarters, accommodations, and vehicle mechanisms for driving. Here is a list of the different vehicles that are often referred to as RVs:

- Caravans

- Coaches

- Campervans

- Motorhomes

- Fifth-wheel trailers

- Popup campers

- Truck campers

All of these different vehicle types function as part vehicle and part home. Some of these vehicles, such as motorhomes, are self-propelled RVs that offer mobile living situations. In comparison, caravans, also called travel trailers or camper trailers, need to be attached to another vehicle and are pulled with a tow. Which RV is right for you ultimately depends on your ideal living situation, how long you will be on the road and your budget.

The RV types listed above have further classifications. Motorhomes, for instance, are separated into Class A, B, and C. The motorhome size determines the class. Once again, you will want to consider your unique situation when determining which class of motorhome is best for you.

In Chapter 3, I will go into more detail about your different RV options. For the purposes of this chapter, you just have to understand that an RV is a vehicle that contains both living and vehicle accommodations and that there are many types of RVs. Later in this book, I will help you determine which RV type is best for your needs.

What Does RV Camping Entail?

Now that you actually know what an RV is, what exactly is RV camping? RV camping allows you to enjoy the benefits of camping while enjoying the benefits of a home. On the one hand, you will still get to sleep in a bed and have access to amenities like air conditioning. On the other hand, you will get to enjoy camping locations in nature and possibly go off the grid.

How it works is that you prep your RV with the amenities of a home. Most RVs are equipped with beds, small kitchen units, tables, air conditioning, and heat. Some will even offer a small bathroom, TV, and more luxury amenities. Prep your RV just like you would your home. Make sure to pack bedding, pillows, towels, cleaning supplies, cookware, space heaters, and laundry bags. Prepping your RV will ensure you get to enjoy the benefits of being at home while out on the road.

From there, you will drive your RV to a location of your choosing. Some RVs will have the home amenities and vehicles in one. Other RVs will need to be attached to the vehicle via a tow and towed to your location. In either case, the RV will basically act as a home on wheels. You will have all of the amenities you packed, but you will be able to take them to new destinations around the nation.

There are plenty of locations to choose from when RV camping. There are some campsites dedicated to RVs exclusively. RV campsites are not necessarily the most picturesque, but they can allow you to unwind and provide you access to electricity and water hookups so you can still enjoy the maximum benefits of modern living while on the road. Many traditional campsites also offer RV spots. These campsites might not have all the electricity and water hookups of RV campsites, but they will likely be more picturesque and settled in the woods.

Of course, you can also find off-the-grid primitive campsites. These campsites are suitable for RV camping, but they are not equipped with any type of electricity or water hookups. Some campsites will not even have flush toilets, showers, or other amenities either. These campsites will be the most picturesque, but they will be the most off the grid as well.

While at the destination of your choosing, you will get to kick back and relax. During the day, you can explore nature, soak in the scenes, and relax outdoors. Come nighttime; you will have a comfortable bed that you can sleep in that is even equipped with locking doors and an AC unit for a comfortable and safe camping experience.

How long you are on the road ultimately depends on you. Some people like to escape for the weekend and find a local RV park in their area. Other people enjoy stopping around partial hookup campsites for months at a time. Others live entirely off the grid by visiting partial campsites for possibly years at a time. The beauty is that it is up to you to determine how long you are on the road. You can enjoy RV camping for as long or short as you deem appropriate.

Part-Time vs. Full-Time RV Living

As mentioned above, it is up to you to determine how long you stay in your RV. You may only be interested in RV camping on occasion, such as on holidays. Other people choose to stay in their RV for an extended amount of time. For instance, some stay in their RV during the summer months and live in their RV part-time as a result. Others live full-time in their RV 365 days out of the year. It is critical to know the differences between part-time and full-time RV living so you can create the best plan based on your lifestyle and needs.

Let us start by digging apart full-time RV living. Full-time RV living is pretty much what it sounds like. It is whenever you live on the road full-time. Your RV is essentially your actual home on the road. Full-time living allows you to live off the grid and enjoy a lifestyle that is constantly changing and moving. It is best suited for singles or young couples who can work on the road but who also want to experience all that life has to offer.

In comparison, part-time RV living is whenever you live on the road for a good chunk of the year. Part-time RV living is different from vacationing in your RV because you are usually on the road for weeks or months at a time, but you are not actually living in your RV either. You have another home that you live in more frequently.

It can be difficult to properly define the difference between part-time and full-time living for insurance policies. Individual insurance policies will have a set amount of time you have to be on the road for it to count as full-time living. In general, you are considered to be living in your RV full-time if you are in your RV for 150 days or more. You will have to actually check with your insurance company to learn what their definition is, but most companies follow this 150-day rule.

There are actually a lot of pros and cons to both full-time and part-time living. On the one hand, full-time living allows you to enjoy nature on the go. You do not have a regular nine to five. Instead, you can enjoy the entire United States by living in your home on wheels. However, it is not without its faults. You have to have a job that you can do remotely, and you will not always have access to Wi-Fi or cell service. You also will not have stable neighbors, and you will have to thoroughly prep to ensure a safe and comfortable full-time RV camping experience.

As for part-time living, there are pros and cons to it as well. It will allow you to enjoy the benefits of both living and a stable home and exploring the world through RV living. You will still be able to actually see your friends and family consistently, and you will have a place to go if you do not feel like staying in your RV. That being said, part-time living can sometimes be more expensive since you have to pay for rent or mortgage on your stable home, in addition to the gas and resources associated with your mobile home.

You need to think carefully about how much you want to be on the road versus how much you want to be at home. If you are not interested in renting or owning a home at all and want to be on the road 24/7, become a full-time RV camper. However, select part-time camping if you already have a home, want the option to go home, and do not view 24/7 RV life as an ideal lifestyle for you.

RV Living vs. Living in a Home: How They Are Different and How They Are Similar

Even though RV living allows you to have a home on the road, living in an RV is very different from living in a home. Although there are some similarities, there are some major differences to be aware of. It is important that you read through the similarities and differences between RV living and living in a home to decide if RV living is right for you.

Similarities

Regardless of whether you live in an RV or in a house, both structures will be your home. This is the most significant similarity between RV living and living in a home. Not to mention, both options will provide you a comfortable bed and a safe place to relax.

In some cases, you may even have access to electricity, running water, and a full-functioning bathroom in an RV. This is not the case for all RVs, but many people who live in full-time RVs equip their RVs with these functionalities to have the same amenities in the RV at home. As a result, you will actually be able to enjoy the luxuries of modern living in both RVs and houses.

Differences

Even though an RV will provide you the same home experience and general amenities as a house, there are quite a few differences between RV living and living in a house. Obviously, living in an RV means you can live anywhere and enjoy beautiful views from your window. With a home, you will be stuck in one place and have one view.

When you live in an RV, your space is very limited, so you will not have much extra storage space. If you are someone who likes to spread out and have a lot of space, RV living may not be for you. In comparison, living in a home provides much more space to walk around, stretch, and move. You will also have more space for storage.

You have to consider the fact that you will not actually have access to the same amenities as a house at all times. Depending on where you are at or the setup of your RV, you might not have constant access to running water or electricity. Furthermore, you will not always have access to an Internet connection, Wi-Fi, or cell service.

Upkeep is vastly different between a house and an RV as well. With a house, you mainly need to focus on cleaning and hire a maintenance professional if something breaks. With an RV, maintenance is 24/7 to ensure it runs properly. You will have to repeatedly get more gas, change filters, and change oil, all in addition to regular maintenance and upkeep like cleaning.

The last major difference between living in an RV and living in a house is the difference in price. For some people, living in an RV is cheaper, whereas living in a home is cheaper for others. Whenever you live in an RV, you do not have to worry about mortgage payments, rent, or other monthly fees. You will have to pay for the vehicle itself, which can be very pricey. For both options, you will have to pay for electricity, but electricity in an RV is normally cheaper than that in a home.

Things to Consider Before Going Off-Grid in an RV

If you are most interested in RV living because you want to go off the grid, there are some things you actually need to consider beforehand. Just actually like everything else in this world, there are pros and cons to going off the grid in an

RV. You will want to consider the pros, cons, and tips before deciding to go off the grid in a recreational vehicle.

Pros and Cons of Going Off-Grid in an RV

The benefits of going off the grid in an RV are pretty obvious. You will be able to sustain yourself without reliance on provided amenities. As a result, you will actually be able to enjoy electricity and water, no matter where you are located. Creating your own electricity can be more affordable in the long run.

There are also some downsides to going off the grid in your RV. At first, it will be more expensive just because you will need to buy the resources in order to go off the grid. At least the resources are long-lasting and allow your RV to generate electricity and other resources without paying for it. You also will need to know some technical know-how in order to set up your off-grid RV.

Arguably, the most overlooked downside of going off grid in an RV is that the tools required for going off-grid are heavy. When living in an RV, you must consider how much weight the vehicle can stand. The more tools you add for off-grid upkeep, the less weight you will actually be able to store in the vehicle in other ways. So, you need to take careful notice of how heavy the off-grid tools are and how much weight your vehicle can hold.

Chapter 2.   Why RV Living?

In this chapter, you will look at why you might want to live in an RV. You will also look at what exactly is defined as "RV Living." While many of you have come to this book knowing what RV living is, chances are more than a few of you are here out of curiosity as well. Maybe you've thought about getting an RV but didn't know it was a viable lifestyle choice. Or maybe you're just tired of the daily grind and are looking at as many options for alternative living situations as possible.

Spoiler: You've happened upon my favorite.

You'll also take some time to explore the growing movement of people who are choosing RV living over the traditional system. We'll see what led them to make their decision and how they feel after making the leap. Finally, we will also look at the pros and cons of RV living.

What is RV Living?

When it comes to RV living there are two key styles of living which it refers to. These are part-time RV living and full-time RV living. While both will be discussed for the first part of the book, chapter five will see us transition into discussing just full-time RV living. You now know there are two kinds of RV living, but what do they mean?

Part-time RV living refers to people who divide their time between living in an RV and living in a house, apartment, or condo. Those who live the part-time RV life tend to either live it during the summer or the winter, either to make use of the nice weather for traveling or to escape from the icy cold of winter. These people live in their RVs for more than just the weekends or a week or two out of the year (those would be recreational RVers). Instead, part-time RVer still lives out of the RV for a longer period of time but they have a place to return to at the end of it.

In contrast, full-time RV living refers to those who spend the whole year in the RV. This doesn't mean that the full-time RVer doesn't own a house or condo, however. They may have a property that they rent out or loan to friends and family, or maybe they hire someone to check on periodically. Full-time RV living isn't necessarily about getting rid of your house; it's about getting out on the road and living adventurously.

And that's it. It's pretty simple, but the effects it has on your lifestyle, happiness, ability to break free from debt, and the sense of adventure it can bring into your life make it so much more than a simple than that. To get a sense of the freedom the RV lifestyle brings with it, let's look at the growing movement of people that have made the transition to see their reasons and their reactions.

The Growing Movement

As you saw above, according to the Washington Post there are already a million Americans who have chosen the RV lifestyle. While some of these people do it because they can't afford traditional living, the fact remains that most of these people are RV living by choice. To say this movement is taking off is an understatement: 2017 set the record for RV sales and the number of households with RVs jumped from 7.5 million in 2005 to 10.5 million. Additionally, RVs are now primarily purchased by people under the age of 45, where previously they were a luxury for after retirement.

You've already seen some reasons people make this choice. The idea of freedom, adventure, and escaping of debt. But these are abstract concepts. The freedoms offered may seem logical but what does that really mean? It's just a claim. So instead of throwing making more claims, let's instead look at what some real people have said about their own transitions to RV living.

They wanted to spend more time with their kids but how could they? They had to work constantly to keep up with all the bills. When Robert got offered a new job in Atlanta, the family didn't feel they had enough money for a traditional house and so they made the jump into RV living with their children and pets.

So how did they find the transition? When interviewed, Jessica warned that it wasn't all fun and games. She mentioned the family has to use a laundromat now and there are just as many chores on the road as there are at home. But she also pointed out that it gives them the freedom to travel as they want. They can set up on a mountain one day, by a beach the next, and find a spot in the woods the day after. That freedom, according to Jessica, makes all the difference to them as a family. They love the lifestyle so much that they even began a YouTube channel called Exploring the Local Life, in which they talk about their experiences and try to inspire others to take up the RV lifestyle.

They aren't the only couple who love the lifestyle. Joyce Ann Seid and Steve Seid got into RVing back in 2001 when they bought one to take trips on the weekends. Within nine years, they transitioned to full-time RV living. They first rented out their house and got a bigger RV, then they realized they liked the new RV so much they transitioned to full-time RV living. They remodeled the interior so that Joyce had a home office to write from. They love the lifestyle, Steven calling it a great life and noting how many nice people they have met in their travels.

The Pros and Cons of RV Living

While I will say again and again that I love and have found joy and positivity in the RV lifestyle, I won't lie and say that there aren't cons as well. This lifestyle isn't right for everyone. But with over a million Americans making the switch, it seems to be right for many people.

Life is about balance. When you are beaten down by the daily grind of existence you don't truly jibe with, then your lives aren't in balance. There is something missing and it leaves us feeling a hole, a lack of… something. You might not be able to identify it easily because you live with it every day. But you feel it and you know something needs to change. I believe that the pros on this list show that RV living can be a way of filling that hole.

Pro: RV living offers a sense of mobility.

In the traditional system, you wake up in your bed at home. You drive to work, do your job and then drive back home to the same neighborhood. Maybe you drive the same route back that you took to work. You get familiar with seeing the same things, over and over again.

It gets to become boring, doesn't it? There is no freedom: only repetition. Maybe you are able to get out on the weekends for a short day trip or stay in another town for a night. But by Sunday it is time to drive home and prepare yourself for work the next morning. The sense of mobility you have is tempered by the demands of the traditional lifestyle.

RV living completely rewrites this story. As you saw Jessica mention above, one night you may stay next to a mountain, the next a forest, a lake, the ocean, the woods. Every single day in an RV gives you the option to up and leave, to find a new place that intrigues you, a new location you want to explore and add its natural wonder to your life experience. Not that it always has to be natural landscapes, either. There are plenty of places in cities that offer free parking, even to RVs. If you wanted you could drive city to city, using your RV to make sure you always have a room.

Con: RV living offers tighter spaces than houses or apartments.

When it comes to RV living, you get used to tight quarters. There isn't much room in 395-square foot RV compared to a one-story house. An RV is roughly the size of a bachelor or studio apartment on wheels. This means that things can start feeling cramped if you don't learn to cut down on your possessions.

It also means that there isn't much space to find a place of your own if you and your family or partner get into a fight. No matter where you are, you are always within spitting distance of the driver and anyone else. This can be a powerful tool for learning how to deal with conflicts, or it can cause damage to your relationship.

With so little space, any amount of mess will make the living space feel like a pigsty. When you have all the space of a house, some clutter and mess happens and is easy to ignore. Your kid's room might be dirty but you keep up with the rest of the place. Or maybe you don't like doing the dishes so you let them build up until you're forced to do them. That's easy to do in a house; you just hang out in the living room rather than the kitchen. But in an RV any amount of mess takes up a much larger percentage of space and will seem much bigger in comparison. This can actually be a real pain, but can also serve as a learning tool to build cleaner habits, too.

Pro: You don't take anything for granted.

At home, you have ready access to the internet, hot water with the turn of a knob, dishwashers, showers, cable tv. They are the things you actually take for granted living in a sedentary lifestyle. All of that changes once you hit the road.

Parks will vary in the quality of their wifi. Clothes will have to be washed in laundromats. Showers have to be planned. Water takes time to heat up. It really promotes a different way of thinking about the services and conveniences available.

But this serves to make you mindful about what you have, not taking anything for granted. When you have to plan out your route so you can hit a shower and laundromat, you become conscious the value these amenities bring to your life. Not only do you become more aware of them, but you develop compassion towards those who lack those same conveniences. Until you know what it takes to get your laundry done without having a machine readily available, you can only look at someone without access and see how dirty they are. But knowing the struggle, you can understand them better and that allows us to care more. In this way, you learn not to take anything for granted and to care more about your fellow man.

Con: Controlling your climate.

This particular con is not unique to RVs alone. How many summer days have you sat inside with the fan on, just hoping and praying that you cool off? However, it can be even harder to control the temperature of an RV than a home.

Opening up the windows can let air in but lets out the AC. The AC can be put on full blast but makes you eat through money. You can set up a fan but considering the small space, it cannot be a very big or powerful one. This can make RV living a particularly sweaty experience during the summer months.

In winter it can also be a challenge to keep warm. Blankets and sweaters make it a lot easier to feel comfortable but they don't always get the job done. You're back to blasting the heat and spending money. Cold or warm drinks and experimentation will help you find your own methods of climate control, but this takes time and the early days of RV living may be uncomfortable.

Pro: Financial Freedom

One of the absolute biggest benefits of RV living is the financial freedom that it offers. Of course, it still requires money to buy the RV, keep it in good shape, eat, do laundry, buy fuel. But even with a list that long, you will still spend significantly less each month than you would with a mortgage.

The price of an RV is much lower than a house, so right out of the gate you spend much less than you would buying a home. Repairs suck, but how many times have you had to get a plumber or electrician into your place to fix some issue? Maybe a clogged pipe or some faulty wiring. Not only are these costly repairs common problems with houses, but faulty wiring could lead to an electrical fire that could see everything you own lost! That's much worse than having to replace some brake pads or even one of the major components like the radiator.

If your house did go up in a fire, you can expect to lose all of the material goods you have accumulated over the years and kept inside it. However, an RV is a much smaller space and promotes a less materialistic lifestyle. Living less a materialistic life means you aren't spending as much money on physical possessions. The RV lifestyle promotes living for experiences, not for possessions.

Pro: Make friends everywhere you go.

If there is one common thread in the experiences hundreds of RVers have reported, it is that you meet just the coolest and nicest people through this lifestyle. Everyone seems to have such unique and crazy stories and they always have a friendly smile for you. You're not just meeting people from the same region you grew up. You are meeting people who have traveled all across the country or sometimes those on vacation exploring a new country. It really is a fantastic way to be exposed to a variety of cultures and add spice to life.

Con: You leave friends behind.

This is the flip side of the last pro. Because this is a more nomadic lifestyle, you are likely to leave your new friends behind. Or have them leave you, as they are also RV living. This means that while you meet many awesome people, you don't get as close to them as you do to your friends in a sedentary lifestyle.

But this doesn't mean that you can't make awesome and close friends. With the internet, you have social networks to keep up with people more easily. This means that despite the distance, you can stay in touch and you can even plan to meet up at certain locations. You might even decide to take a trip together and set a shared route.

Summary

- RV living refers to either the part-time or full-time habitation of an RV.

- There are over a million Americans that have transitioned to RV living and that number is still growing.

- RV living offers an alternative lifestyle to the traditional white picket fence American dream of owning a house.

- Living in an RV is actually a way to get mobility and adventure back into your life because you are never stuck in a single location.

- Living in an RV means living in a tighter space and this can be difficult to adapt to at first.

- Because we're always on the road and don't have the same utilities you have when you own a home, living an RV teaches you not to take anything for granted and this helps you to grow in compassion.

- It can be tough figuring out how to control the climate of an RV during those hot summer days and cold winter nights.

- But living in an RV means you don't have to spend money on a mortgage and the cost of housekeeping, so it can be a great way to get the financial freedom to pay your debts off and take control of your earnings.

- You meet all kinds of wonderful and unique people living the RV lifestyle, people from all over the country and world.

- The nomadic aspect of RV living means you also have to leave those people behind, or that they leave you behind, but with the technology age, it's easier than ever to stay in touch with your new friends.

In the next parts, you will eventually learn how to find the RV that is perfect for you. This chapter will look at what you should know before purchasing, whether you want to purchase used or new, what kind of repairs and maintenance you can expect after buying, and how to make sure that the RV that you bought is as perfect as you dreamed it would be.

Chapter 3.   Understanding RV Terminology

As a newbie in this awesome and adventurous world, you will realize that there are certain slang words that RV campers use when interacting with each other. Sometimes, even a camper who has been on the journey for years may find a new slang word that they have never heard or used before. However, experienced RV campers may take a wild guess and get the meaning of the word right.

So what are these words, and what are their meanings?

Below are some general phrases and words used in the RV world that can help you when purchasing an RV. These words will also help you when interacting with fellow RV owners, as well as speaking about your RV issues to your insurance company.

With knowledge of this lingo, you may influence people into thinking that you are an experienced, full-time RV camper, even if you are a beginner. I hope this will help you in talking to other people in the RV world.

Basement – This is the area used for storage. This area is under your motorhome's main area and is accessed from outside. These areas are normally in class A or Class C motorhomes.

Chucking - This is a back and forth movement that is usually violent. It is encountered when towing and normally generated if the trailer is unbalanced or moving on a bumpy road.

Toad (Dinghy) – This term describes the vehicle being towed by your motorhome.

Coach - This is another name for the Class A RV.

Chassis – This stands for the frame that holds the entire RV.

Extended Stay Site - this is the campsite where campers stay for a long time. Some stay in these camps for months and others for a whole season.

Black Water Tank – This is the place where the wastewater in the RV is held.

Blue Boy - These are wheeled plastic totes that are portable. They are normally used to move the waste tank sewage from the trailer to the dumpsite. It is normally towed by the tow vehicle at a very slow speed.

Boondocking / Dry camping – Also known as "roughing it," boondocking is camping without any external hookups or resources, like electricity, sewer, and water.

Fiver – This is another name for a 5th wheel RV.

Dump Station – This is the place where the black and grey tanks are emptied.

Fresh Water Tank – This is where drinking water is kept.

Cockpit – This is the driver's seat at the motorhome, the spot where he or she drives from.

Dually – This is a tow vehicle that is light-duty or a pickup truck. Its rear axle usually has four tires.

Full Hookup- This is a campsite with all the resources needed, like sewage, water, and electricity.

Full-Timers – These are campers that live the RV lifestyle throughout the year.

Batwing - This is the name used for the TV antenna in standard RVs. These antennas resemble a pair of wings.

Holding Tanks – This describes the three distinct water tanks that most motorhomes have. These are the fresh, grey, and black tanks.

Galley - This is the other name for the kitchen.

Hula Skirt – This is a skirt that is installed at a motorhome's back bumper. It is important as it helps stop trash that is discharged from the rear wheels from causing damage to the vehicles following the motorhome.

Gray Water Tank – This is the place where water used from showers and sinks is deposited.

King Pin - This piece attaches to the clamps of the 5th wheel block at the rear of the tow vehicle.

Newbie - This is someone new to the trailer world

Hose Bib - A campsite tap with clean water.

Part-Timers – These are people who still have a permanent place of residence, but live a few months of the year in their RV.

Honey Wagon - A trailer or truck with a big liquid tank on top of it. This tank usually goes around places pumping out the waste tanks on RVs.

Jake Brake - This is the engine brake which is used on some diesel-powered vehicles.

Puller – This is a Class A Diesel RV with a diesel motor placed at the front.

Sani-Dump - This is the other name for a sewer dump station. It is where campers empty their trash tanks.

Slideout – This is an RV feature that opens up to generate more space for living. It is normally found in the bedroom and living rooms.

Snowbirds – These are people who love to go south with their RVs during wintertime. During the summer, they usually go north.

Sticks N Bricks - This is the name for a regular kind of permanent home.

Stinky Slinky- This is what is also known as the flexible sewer hose. It is used to drain the waste tanks of the RV.

Genset - This is the electric generator used in most motorhomes.

Reefer - This refers to the electric refrigerator or the LP gas.

Tail Swing - This term is used to describe the additional distance at the RV's rear end, which is used when making a turn. When the space between the RV end and the rear wheel is longer, the tail swing will also be larger. When turning corners in a cramped location, it is vital that you have an idea of the state of your tail swing.

Pusher – These are Class A diesel-powered RVs that have the diesel motor positioned at the rear.

Triple Tow - This is the courageous act of towing your RV plus an extra trailer behind it — for instance, an RV and a boat.

Pull-Through – This is a campsite with ample entrance and exit that make it possible for campers to set up and move on without always having to line up.

Rig – This is another name for a motorhome.

Wheel Chocks - These are slanted blocks, which are normally manufactured from plastic materials. They can also sometimes be made from wood. They keep the RV from rolling.

Workamping - This is the name used to describe campers who do work free work at campsites and the benefits they receive. They are sometimes paid a small wage. This is something that full-timers do to cut down on living costs.

Tow Dolly - This is a two-wheeled trailer that is small in size. They are used for attaching a tow vehicle to the rear end of an RV.

RBR - This is an abbreviation for Really Big Rig.

VBR - This is an abbreviation for Very Big Rig.

Wally Dock - This is a term used by seasoned RV users to describe overnight parking of your RV at Walmart

Chapter 4.   Before You Get Started

Now that that's over with and you feel like you are up to the task, you need to manage your expectations about the demands of RV life. Don't get us wrong - this is totally not to dissuade you, but more along the lines of letting you know the realities of living in an RV or any mobile home, for that matter. We hope this can give you a true inside peek at how we full-timers live our lives before you decide to embark on your own journey. Going in with the right expectation and mindset can actually make your life out here more fruitful in the long run, so let's get to it!

Live Purposely and Don't Be Wasteful

This is something we keep on telling our children too. It's important to be mindful of the little things, like picking up after yourselves and doing things deliberately and with purpose so that everything you do is not wasteful. I feel like you have to be very disciplined when you live in such a small space. Every night you need to sweep, clean, and put things back in order, especially if you have transforming furniture, like when your counter space also turns into a bed or a sitting space. You have to do due diligence, or else your whole rig will just be chaos, and you'll have to wade through your things day in and day out - you might just get featured in an episode of "Hoarders" if you're not careful.

As such, your cleaning routine will change. If in your stick-and-bricks home you can clean once a week or twice a month, with such a small space, things that are not organized and thrown around haphazardly will accumulate and make your space even smaller. Of course, with kids, it's even harder - chores should be divided, and I enforce the clean-as-you-go rule strictly. Keep the clothes stored away. Simple cleanups at the end of each day will keep your RV spic and span without much effort.

My husband and I were not even the eco-friendly sorts when we started on this journey, but a year in, we started unconsciously living a semi "zero waste" lifestyle and, by default, being more eco-friendly. When you're on the road with no place to throw your trash out, you'd be lugging around a few days' worth of dirty clothes and waste. And trust me, keeping stinky trash with you in such a small space, even with all your vents, fans, and windows opened, can make your house stink. Even cooking with a lot of spices can make our bed smell like garlic for a few days - not to mention that if you have a smaller rig, even your grey water tank will start smelling after a few days.

And even before living minimally was a thing, we lot have been Marie Kondo-ing our whole home for years. Out here, you need to ask yourself, "What are my bare minimum requirements to survive? What do I need around me to function like a human being every day? Do I really need this?" If not, it has no place in your RV.

Travel with Someone You Can Get Along With

Think of it this way: when you're traveling in an RV, there's really no escape from your travel companion, is there? Living in an RV will test the relationship to the limit - you must learn to give in and compromise whenever possible. We've heard a lot of sad stories where couples break up, and even YouTuber couples calling it quits after a measly year of traveling. We've even heard of a family totally giving up the RV life to go back to their stick-and-stones to save their relationship.

So communication is the absolute key to making this work - being cooped up for hours on end inside your RV can take a toll on most relationships. And if you suddenly want to take up traveling with your partner and kids, remember that you shouldn't force your children or anyone else for that matter to comply with your decision. It's hard to enjoy what's out here if you have a grumbling teen unwillingly stuck with you all the way. So make sure you talk and plan it out with your travel companions.

As for the kids, don't ever uproot them from their schools and friends. It will be hard to move around for children; this is especially true for most teens and adolescents. Our kids are pretty young right now, and we're glad that they're enjoying this certain chapter of their lives out here. My husband would always say that maybe this part of their life will be something that they won't even remember that much - maybe just a fleeting memory of happiness, curiosity, and adventure at the back of their minds that can hopefully stay with them as they grow up. That said, this RV life, however great it sounds like, can be a bit taxing for relationships, so it's always good to be considerate of your companions.

Evaluate Your Reason for Choosing this Lifestyle

Recently, we've seen a new wave of people living the RV life for all the wrong reasons, like becoming a YouTube star or Instagram famous. Now, I'm not raining on anyone's parade here - there are a lot of happy RV campers out here doing YouTube full time or on the side. Heck, we even upload a few videos of our own! So I totally have nothing against social media influencers here, but let me just share with you a little conversation we had with a young couple we met while on the road to the coast.

They said they jumped into this life with the intent of recording it and sharing it on social media, thinking that could be their source of income. But in the end, they said, they had to ask themselves, are they living for their life on the road? Or are they living for themselves?

Making this life the whole content of your channel can bring you followers, for sure. But in the end, it's going to get tiring, and you would ask yourself, will your subscribers still follow you if you gave up on this kind of life? How about your income then? You then get tied to this life with no way out unless you look for another way to earn your keep. You will definitely feel miserable if you compare your life to theirs, so you must understand that an influencer's job is to romanticize life in general. They're not going to show you the realities of living the RV life on the road.

You Will Get Tired of Traveling

If you're thinking that there's just no possible way anyone will ever get tired of traveling, think again - remember the last time you went on a trip. It was fun and all, but when you got home, didn't you feel just so exhausted from all that excitement and adrenaline that you just wanted to curl up and sleep for a few days to rest?

Traveling full time will be very tiring. It's quite inaccurate if you picture yourself going on great adventures every day because I'm telling you right now that you definitely will have lazy days where you will want to just "stay in." You'll find yourself just sitting inside your RV to work or to rest - only going out to pee and to look for something to eat - this applies if you only have a very basic rig that consists only of you, your car, and your bed.

Travel burnout is a thing, and being on the road for years will leave you drained, emotionally and physically. We've seen foreign travelers in Thailand who just spend all day inside their hostel doing nothing - it seems like they've lost that sense of curiosity and wonder that you need with you when you travel.

And so you need to strike a balance between resting and moving, which is going to be hard when your mindset is forced to think that you need to be constantly on the move, especially when your house basically moves with you. But doing so will only lead you to think of your "moving around" as a chore; therefore, your rests will just keep getting longer. See the dilemma here? So you'll think, "I'll just keep on going then." But then the rests are also needed for you to recharge. As I said before, being constantly on the move will be very tiring, and when everyone is tired, tensions will rise.

I will tell you that there are times when we just park our rig in our parents' house or even at our friend's house for a couple of days and weeks just to have a break - this is what we call "moochdocking." Or even splurge a bit and check in to a nice hotel to take a break from all that cleaning, organizing, and traveling to refresh our minds. We find ourselves being able to think more clearly, and things just fall into place after.

They travel non-stop for 2 to 3 months and then pick a place where they can stay or park for just a month to rest up and plan things for the next leg of their journey. Some also stay stationary in their RVs during a certain season and only start traveling when it's "their" season. It's kind of like the migration of birds, my husband would joke. It's staying inside during winter and moving when it's summer - or vice versa, staying inside during the summer and moving only in the winter to escape the cold (this type of RVer is called a "snowbird").

The World Wide Web

Internet technology is great overall, but there will be dead spots all over the country. You will find yourself climbing up rocks and your rig just to get a signal sometimes. This is especially true if you love to go boondocking. But hey, two birds in one stone! Hiking plus cell reception!

With both of us working full time in our rig, we really need our internet to work as smoothly as possible. There's a couple of really great internet service providers out there, and we find ourselves covered - most of the time - with a wireless hotspot and the mobile data from our phones. That's more or less around 55 GB of data per month. If we go through all that, we'll still have internet, but the speeds tend to slow down by a lot. A lot of RVers also use Wi-Fi boosters - these are lifesavers, especially if you need to send big files.

Starbucks is also an option! But kidding aside, it's true that a lot of RVers with smaller rigs tend to go to coffee shops for Wi-Fi. Think of it this way - you're back in civilization, you get good coffee and pastries, and the internet speeds are great. Some people we know who do YouTube full time actually schedule their trips so that they find themselves in a city or near a city in time to upload new videos. Uploading videos with one bar of the internet brings you back to the '90s with speeds that can rival dial-up systems. And as you start to travel around, you would begin to take note of campsites with good reception. Because - and I'm not ashamed to say this - internet is life.

Mail and Deliveries

Ah, the deliveries. One thing I really miss is our deliveries and the convenience of it - can't really call Uber Foods when you're craving that really scrumptious squid ink pasta you had last week because you're out here in your rig halfway across the state. You can still technically get goods delivered - we do it all the time, by the way: spare parts for the rig, medicine prescription for our kid (yes, you can get them delivered - more on that later), and sometimes these cute little bowls from Anthropologie. Splurge, I know.

You just need to find campsites that will accept and hold the deliveries for you. For this, you need to schedule and time your trips, so when you get to a certain campsite - fingers crossed - your deliveries will be waiting for you. Another option is post offices. You can get your mail delivered to post offices, but again, as with campsites, not all post offices will accept general deliveries.

Timing and scheduling are everything with mails and deliveries. But luckily for us, most mail can now be diverted to emails, so that's one less thing to worry about.

Basic Necessities

RV technology has improved a lot since decades ago. Before, you couldn't even think of bringing with you a shower, a toilet, a fridge, or even a stove. Back in the RV's early years, the setup was spartan at most. You carry along tents, sleeping bags, and other camping equipment such as coolers and a mini stove. And with the years came more additions to this humble "camping trailer": collapsible tents, sleeping spaces, drawers, and cupboards, transforming into a perfect little home away from home for our countrymen who are craving to be back or one with nature.

These days, you'll see hundreds of different RV technology being developed, from big companies to small independent players. You can now have your choice of different kinds of toilets to bring with you depending on your needs. There are even movable ones, so you can store them in your shower to save space. Or how about a hydraulic bunk bed installed in your camper van for extra sleeping space?

All these sound nifty, but not everything will be as easy as when you live in an actual house. It doesn't matter if the toilet you picked to bring with you on your journey is the most expensive one in the market - at the end of the particular day, you will still have to empty the tank or the holding bin out. Due to this, some RVers will often resort to option number 1, which is to hide between the bushes with a shovel. This is to either save water and electricity or stretch the time in between clearing out the tanks - because, let's face it, no one wants to clean out the tanks.

On electricity, there are different ways on how to get power inside your RV. Most big rigs have generator sets or gensets inside, but you also have a choice between solar panels, batteries, and gasoline. On solar panels, you are basically at the mercy of the weather - if it's cloudy and stormy most of the week, then get ready to live with your flashlight. Alternatively, you can just follow the sun, but only if you're willing to compromise your schedule.

You also have the option of bringing a secondary battery or a mini Genset with you. You can charge your batteries using your vehicle's alternator - your vehicle needs to be moving, though, or else you'd be draining your vehicle's main battery, and then you can't even start your car. You can also use RV hookups at a campsite - depending on how you travel, this, for us, is the best option. You can also use gasoline to power your generators, but then again, you need to lug along jugs of highly flammable liquid in your car. Coupled with a propane stove, that can spell trouble if not used correctly. RVers with these types of hookups usually have carbon dioxide and other gas monitors installed around their RV for safety.

The bottom line is that if you're not parked in a campsite and hooked up to shore power - that's electricity connected to the grid - then you need to conserve electricity or at least monitor your usage. And it's best to bring with you lithium batteries and flashlights for emergencies because you never know.

The same goes with water - unless you're in a campsite and hooked up to the camp's water supply (and sewer), you will be using your rig's water tanks. Your usage will depend on how big of a tank you can fit in under there. To save water, there are a few manufacturers out there that offer mechanisms that recycle shower water using a filtration system. This, of course, can only be used to shower; water for your sink would be coming from another tank. But still, you won't have an unlimited supply of water in your tank, so shower times are limited to minutes - no long luxurious baths here.

Laundry is also best done when your RV is hooked up, especially if you have a washing machine with you. A single to two loads can fill up your grey water tank so fast you won't be able to use your sink, shower, or your toilet anymore. And since we all know how fast dirty clothes can accumulate, it would be best to do your laundry every time you see a laundromat. So keep a bucket of coins with you at all times.

In a nutshell, your access to power and water is limited at most. So it's best to keep them in mind at all times, lest you wake up one day and your fridge just defrosted itself because your battery ran out - this happened to us a lot in our first year, so lesson learned.

Chapter 5.   How to Choose an RV?

RVs are a boon for frequent campers as they allow you to travel and camp in great comfort. An RV allows families and friends to spend quality time together. It is cost-effective as compared to planes, and the experience cannot be compared with anything else. It puts you right in the heart of nature without forgoing certain modern amenities and comforts. This is why nowadays people prefer using RVs as compared to traditional tents and paraphernalia.

Another positive aspect of RVs is that they offer people freedom. They allow you to choose your vehicle, your destination, and your schedule, as well. Freedom is a brilliant aspect, but it can be overwhelming, as well. For instance, when we are offered a lot of choices in the world, we may get confused about which product is right for us. Similarly, there exist a variety of RVs and similar vehicles, and choosing the best can be difficult.

It will cover all the prominent types and will also cover the benefits and the problems associated with them. This is especially true in the particular case of beginners who often buy incorrect and unsuitable RVs due to a lack of knowledge. Your RV should not be too small or too large, either.

Motorized Vs. Towable RVs

They have engines and can be driven around. A motorized RV is the best of both worlds, as it has to live as well as driving capabilities. You do not need to connect your vehicle to another vehicle just to drive it around. Similarly, you do not need a hitch and unhitch it at the campsite, either. Both the living quarters and engine are located in the same vehicle, and thus, it is easy to maneuver and handle. New drivers are often more comfortable with this kind of set up as compared to towable vehicles because turning and managing two vehicles at the same time is difficult. If you are a beginner, it can even lead to accidents and other such problems. While all the four kinds are considered to be RVs, but there is so much difference between all of them that it can still be a daunting experience to buy one. Let us have a close look at them one by one.

Class A Motorhomes

These are the most common and popular motorized RVs. They are heavy-duty and can endure a lot of wear and tear. They are constructed on specially designed chassis and are the largest of all the RVs. They can range between 21 feet to 50 feet. They often weigh around 20,000 lbs. or more.

They are extremely spacious and roomy. They have great and comfortable living spaces and sleeping accommodations. Normally they can accommodate around ten or more people. Some of them also feature a separate master bedroom section. They can also be extended to expand the living space. Some Class A RVs also have 'basements' where you can store extra products.

The kitchens in these RVs can compete with any decent traditional house kitchen. You can also find gadgets such as icemakers, laundry machines, bathing facilities, and other similar amenities. They are luxurious and allow people to travel and camp in style and comfort.

As these RVs are gigantic, many beginners often tend to avoid them. They are difficult to maneuver, especially on narrow and windy roads. Parking such RVs is pretty difficult, as well. It is almost impossible to drive them through the wilderness for exploration, and many people often take their other vehicles with these RVs for mobility and convenience.

They are expensive and often require a lot of maintenance. They also require a lot of fuel, which can increase prices significantly.

Class B Motorhomes

Class B Motorhomes are also known as van campers. They are smaller than Class A and are easy to drive as they are often built on van chassis.

They are smaller in size, so the living and sleeping spaces too are slightly compact, but what makes these RVs immensely popular is that they are easy to drive. You do not need any extra vehicles as they can be driven around without any problems. This factor makes them great for general excursions and day trips.

These RVs often contain queen size beds, a small kitchen, some 'bath attachments,' and a fair amount of storage space. It is decent for three to four people, but it is best suited for couples.

Class Bs are affordable and require less fuel. They are great for spontaneous travelers.

Class C Motorhomes

Class C Motorhomes are, in a way combination of Class As and Bs. They are versatile and are generally affordable as compared to the other two.

The starting price of these vans is a lover than Class B (but they still manage to provide more amenities). The maintenance and fuel, however, can set you back significantly.

This RV is great for people who are traveling on a budget or for small families. They have all the facilities and amenities and are therefore quite popular with frugal RVers.

Campervans

These are technically Class B RVs. Class B RVs are often called as campervans. But generally, when this word is used, people picture a smaller van, for instance, like the Volkswagen Westphalia.

These are really popular on Instagram due to their looks and panache. They are petite but comfortable and are highly versatile. They provide you style, looks, along with some amenities and small but comfortable living space. It also contains simple cooking facilities, dining area, and sleeping space for one to two people. They rarely feature a bathroom set up. These are small and thus are suitable for weekend gateways. They are also good for solo travelers.

Now, let us look at towable RVs.

Towable RVs

Towable RVs are also known as trailers. They need a tow vehicle to carry them from one place to another. The size of the truck (or the car) depends on the size and the weight of the RV.

What makes Towable RVs so popular is that they are often cheaper as compared to motorized RVs. They do not have any motor, which is why they do not face any engine or other mechanical problems. Once you reach the destination, you can unhitch the trailer from your vehicle and can explore the surrounding with your regular vehicle. There are five different types of Towable RVs; they are fifth-wheel trailers, sport-utility trailers, travel trailers, pop up trailers, and truck campers. Let us actually have a look at them below.

Fifth Wheels

Fifth-wheel trailers are the most luxurious and the largest towable RVs. They are also the most expensive as well.

They are around 20 to 40 feet in size and require large trucks to tow around. They are known as fifth-wheel trailers because a fifth wheel is attached to the tow vehicle. It makes the whole thing stronger as compared to regular ball hitches.

They do not have a cockpit, which provides a lot of space. This extra space is great as it allows these types to have proper and full-sized kitchens, baths, etc. They also have a lot of storage space and can easily adjust at least eight people.

Travel Trailers

These are extremely versatile, and they come in many different sizes and shapes. You can find tiny 4-foot models and also huge 40 feet models with modern amenities.

Like the size variations, the floor plan and the amenities vary as well. For instance, large models often have spacious kitchens, multiple bedrooms, and full baths. The smaller ones rarely have these amenities and often contain only sleeping space for a couple of people. They can be towed around generally by all kinds of vehicles. They use a ball hitch receiver for linking. They are appropriate and well suited for small families.

It is illegal to ride in travel trailers (and fifth-wheels) while in motion. It is thus recommended to tow them with a bigger car or vehicle. Driving around with these attached can be difficult as well, especially in the case of larger models.

Sport-Utility Trailers

Sport-utility trailers are also known as SUTs and toy haulers. They are a new entry in the world of RVs. They have been designed to allow people to transport their motorcycles, jet skis, and other such vehicles with ease. They are normally around 20-35 feet. Their body is divided into two sections - the end with a ramp and the front with living quarters. Almost all the people who use this vehicle use it for its dedicated purpose, but it is possible to use the tail end for extra storage as well. You can convert the end into other areas such as a home office etc. too.

Like other RVs, SUTs too face challenges such as tail swing, poor maneuverability, and limited passenger space. Yet, they are great for people who really want to bring their motorized vehicles with them on vacations.

Truck Campers

These vehicles are not only cost-effective, but they are also easy to drive. They are also known as cab-overs or slide-ins. They are constructed by connecting a hard-sided camper shell to a regular pickup truck.

These are best suited for two to four passengers and have moderate dining, cooking, sleeping, bath, and storage facilities. These RVs are best suited for people who love traveling spontaneously. They are best for those who love the outdoors and are constantly looking for an adventure. They are also great for people who prefer drivability and flexibility to luxury. They are also very affordable. These are compact and still, have a lot of features.

Pop Up Campers

They have immense transforming capabilities and are great for people who love to travel a lot. They are compact and have a lot of extensions to make them comfortable. They normally contain a basic bathroom and kitchen facilities. They can harbor five to six people comfortably. These are well suited for occasional trips. They are meant for long-term living. They do not have a lot of storage. Tent style extensions do not offer a lot of protection from elements. They are lightweight and easy to drive. They can be towed by any simple vehicles, including minivans and SUVs.

Chapter 6.   Best RVs for Winter Living

Not all RVs are suitable for staying in a winter wonderland. Your RV needs certain features that will make it suitable and able to withstand wintry storms and cold.

Certain RVs are specifically designed in such a way that they can withstand even the harshest of temperatures. They can brave snowy conditions and subzero temperatures without cracking a sweat. In this section, let us actually have a look at some of the best winter RVs that will help you travel in style and enjoy warmth and comfort.

Windjammer 3008W Travel Trailer

Features

- Electronically controlled holding tanks

- Total trailer insulation

- Thermo-pane windows

- Fireplace upgrade

- The heated mattress in the master bedroom

- Maxxaire ventilation fan

- Vent cover

- Floor-ducted furnace

Lance 4 Seasons Travel Trailer

Features

- Insulated hatch covers (removable)

- Azdel insulation stops rot, mould, and mildew even if the trailer is exposed to wet conditions for a long time. It also makes the trailer soundproof.

- Water heater bypass

- Ducted heating system

- Dual pane insulated window with soundproofing abilities.

Forest River Arctic Wolf

There are two versions available for this vehicle, let us have a look at the features of both of these versions one by one.

Arctic Package

- Solar wiring and prep

- Upper Bunk Windows

- Outside shower

- Pullout kitchen tap

- Friction hinge doors

Extreme Weather Package

- Racetrack ducted air conditioning

- Arctic insulation

- Quick cool fan

- High circulation ceiling fan

- Insulated upper decking

- Heated underbelly

- Furnace

Jayco 327CKTS Eagle

Optional features include:

- Dry camping package

- Dual pane safety glass windows

- Sani-con turbo waste management system

- Second power awning

Heartland Bighorn

Features

- Furnace

- Insulated A/C duct system

- Single piece under-floor heating duct

Heartland LM Arlington

Features

- Bedroom reading lights

- Power tilt bed

- High rise coffee table

- Safe

- ☐ Stainless steel oven

- ☐ Backlit tile backsplash

- ☐ USB ports

- ☐ Soft tables

- ☐ A multiplex lighting system

- ☐ Along with these, you can also add alumni guard awnings, exterior TV, slide room awnings, bathroom fan, dishwasher, etc.

Northwood Arctic Fox

It is particularly one of the most well-known and often used vehicles for winters.

Features

- ☐ Full tub with hiding away shower screen and bath skylight

- ☐ USB chargers

- ☐ Queen mattress

- ☐ Porcelain toilet with foot pedal

- ☐ Fan vents in the bedroom

- ☐ Shaded skylights in kitchen

- ☐ Extra large fridge

- ☐ Microwave

- ☐ Booth dinner

- ☐ Jackknife sofa with throw pillows

- ☐ Digital thermostat

- ☐ Smoke detectors

- ☐ CO detectors

- ☐ LPG detectors

- ☐ 19 inch LED TV with DVD player and Bluetooth

- ☐ 15-inch aluminum wheels

Keystone Montana

Features

- ☐ Free Flow Air conditioning

- ☐ Dual thermostat

- ☐ Remote sensor with a ducted second A/C

- ☐ 12v tank heaters

- ☐ Heated city water

- ☐ Heated exterior convenience center

- ☐ In-floor water lines

- ☐ Heated underbelly that is enclosed and insulated

- ☐ Dump valves (Insulated and enclosed)

- Holding tanks (Enclosed and insulated)

- Completely vented attic system

- Foam core straight-line heat duct system

- Auto-ignition

- Insulated roof

- Insulated slide-out floors

You can see that there are many different varieties of winter-suitable RVs that can help you stay in a winter/snowy area with ease.

Chapter 7. Points to Remember Before Buying an RV

Buying an RV is not as simple as getting a new car (which is also not a simple decision). There are some essential criteria you actually need to think about. Some people think that considering the below points dashes their hopes of ever owning an RV, but I beg to differ. I think you have to be realistic when you are buying an RV. In fact, this point goes for any big investment you make throughout your life.

Think about it, how long did it take you to decide to buy your home or move into an apartment? You must have checked out the location, price, amenities, accessibility to transportation, internet access, building materials, age of the building, neighborhood, and probably a dozen other factors before you decided to buy, rent, or lease the place.

Let us look at some of the requirements you should actually consider before you decide to buy your RV.

Type of Camping

Think about the type of camping that you would like to do. For the purpose of this book, we are going to assume that you will be in your RV full-time.

However, if you would like to focus on primitive camping, you could think about investing in a travel trailer or a pop-up tent.

For our purpose, however, we are going to be looking at Class As, Class Cs, airstreams, or maybe even vintages—but more on that later in this chapter.

Your Journey

It is important to have a rough idea of the places you would like to travel to. By knowing this, you can understand what kind of RV you would like to get. For example, if you are thinking of staying at public parks, then you should ideally consider getting an RV that is no more than 32 feet. With smaller units, you won't encounter many problems.

If you are thinking of investing in bigger RVs, then you should also think about the stops you are going to make on your journey. Where are some of the ideal places you can do with an RV of the size that you are going to get?

The important thing to remember about this point is that you don't have to get into the details of the journey; that's for another chapter. You are simply developing a rough idea to help you make an appropriate purchase decision.

Stay for Long or Travel Constantly?

The bigger the RV, the more fuel it consumes. This could become an important factor in deciding what kind of RV you would like for longer travels. Furthermore, it is not just about the size, but all the features packed into the vehicle. More electrical components means more fuel for your journey.

On the flipside, if you are planning to stay in one spot for a longer duration, then you should think about what your vehicle can offer you in terms of everyday living requirements.

When you are traveling, you might also want to consider the terrain you may traverse. If you are planning to ride off the beaten track, consider the overall build of the RV. Most vehicles are built low to the ground, which means navigating through uneven terrain may pose as a challenge for your RV. Remember that RV maintenance may be expensive, so damaging it frequently is really going to put a dent in your wallet.

RV Occupants

How many people are going to travel in the RV? Are you going to be bringing any pets? If so, will they need to go outside frequently, or are they just indoor pets? Are kids going to join you in the RV? Do you need a small space for them to play or study?

The above questions will help you choose an RV that offers sufficient space to provide for all your answers. For example, if you have a camper van, then you are not going to be able to fit two dogs and your family, as well.

Your Budget

This is probably something you will be taking into account a lot. To be honest, not many people like thinking about the budget, but it is important to take note of your finances. More importantly, you need to have a realistic projection of your purchase. Let's say you are planning to spend just under $50,000 for an RV because that is all you will require. That's great! Perhaps you are going to be traveling alone and don't need all the extra baggage or people. But then again, after considering all the previous options, you may think of investing in a bigger RV, yet realize you can easily shell out $150,000 (key word here is 'easily') for a well-appointed vehicle. You should not be in a position where you are borrowing money from different sources for your RV. If you are, there is a separate section below for you that you need to take a look at. You might also need to consider the possibility of a fifth wheel and a truck, but more on that in Point #7.

Getting Money

I don't recommend this option. The reason why you are shifting to a mobile home is not just to downsize in reality, but in your life as well. You are minimizing the influence of materialistic objects, living your life to the fullest, and avoiding the stress of bills and debts. If you start borrowing money from the bank or other financial institutions, then your debts will follow you wherever you go. No open space will eliminate the presence of impending loans from your mind.

For your peace of mind, try not to borrow money.

However, an RV is an expensive investment, so I can understand the need to consider financing options. For that reason, here are a few tips to consider:

- Make sure you calculate your loan amount and the monthly payment scheme. When you are calculating this, you need to make it as realistic as possible. Do not try and give yourself wiggle room. This is your future and finances we are talking about, after all.

- When calculating the debt payment scheme, make sure you include all the expenses you might require while using your RV. Do you have enough for the loans you have taken? Can you comfortably pay off what you've borrowed?

- Do not borrow any amount you cannot pay back within two years. I don't recommend working on your loan for more than two years because of the stress it could bring to your life. Think about this way, do you really want to spend more than the first couple of years of your RV life worrying about loans?

- Keep a strict budget during the payment period. Do not overspend when you are living in the RV. Make sure that you prioritize your basic needs first (including fuel for the RV and other such expenses), then focus on your debts, and finally on anything else that you require.

☐ I've said this before and I am going to repeat it again: expect the best and prepare for the worst. What happens during a medical emergency? What about urgent repairs to your RV? Are you able to pay for such expenses and still pay back your debts?

☐ Would you need to invest in a fifth wheel and a truck? If so, are you able to meet those investments and pay off your debts, as well?

As you can see, borrowing money is a pretty tough choice. Make sure you are absolutely certain of your decision. If you think your mind is rather biased towards the idea of a loan because you are tempted to get a fancy RV, then seek advice from your friends, family, or experts in your area. Get a second and also a third opinion before you think about borrowing any money.

Truck

If you are planning to actually get yourself a travel trailer, then you might need a truck or a fifth wheel.

So, what exactly is this 'fifth wheel' we are talking about? It sounds like four wheels are going on a double date, and Mr. Fifth Wheel is all by himself.

That's not the kind of fifth wheel we are talking about, and quite frankly, I think the term 'third wheel' is used for anybody, regardless of how many people they are with.

But I digress; back to the point I am trying to make. A fifth wheel is a coupling mechanism that is used to attach the truck to the trailer.

The above point might be a little confusing, so let me actually break it down for you.

There are two types of travel trailers: those that are attached to the back bumper of a truck, or any other form of towing vehicle, and those attached to the bed of the towing vehicle. A ball-and-coupler hitch mechanism is typically used to attach the trailer to the towing vehicle. A fifth-wheel trailer, on the other hand, is not attached to your rear bumper. Rather, it is connected to the bed of a truck or the towing vehicle using a special jaw hitch. As you can see, if you are getting a travel trailer, then you should ideally have a truck that is big enough to pull it. If you are planning on getting a fifth-wheel trailer, you might need to invest in the fifth wheel mechanism.

Think about this when you are considering your RV choices.

The Driver

This might sound like an odd point to make note of, but trust me when I say that it might be useful in the long run. If you have people traveling with you and would like to share the driving responsibilities with someone else, then you need to get an RV that is convenient for both you and the other person to drive.

If you need to check out how it feels like to be in the RV of your choosing, you can try taking one out for a test run. This will give you a sense of what you are buying, or if you would like to consider a different purchase.

Features

You should ideally think about the features if you have sufficient funds to pay for them, as the more features an RV has, the more expensive it might get. Different RVs provide different features. The best way to choose something that is right for you is to consider your lifestyle. Think of some of the luxuries you used to enjoy and see if you can afford them when it comes to your RV.

Here are a few options you might think about:

- ☐ Television

- ☐ Bunk bed

- ☐ Dining table

- ☐ Washer and dryer

- ☐ Multipurpose areas

- ☐ A desk

- ☐ Basement storage

- ☐ Two bathrooms

Once you have considered the above, and all the other points in this list, then you are able to make an informed decision about your RV.

But while we are actually on the subject of important points to think about, it is time we dispel some myths that have cropped up around RVs and RV lifestyles.

Chapter 8.   What Does It Cost to Live in an RV

This is one of the biggest questions when getting started with an RV live. Without knowing how much it costs to live in an RV, it can be hard to figure out if you can afford it or not. The good news is that there are people from every income level and financial situation who have found a way to make the RV life work for them. If they are careful with their money, most couples and families spend between $2,500 and $3,500 per month.

It's hard to say how much it costs to live in an RV because it depends on so many different things and choices. Most RVers agree that living in an RV will usually cost about the same as what you spend on your regular life.

The amount you will be spending would depend on what you want to do with your RV. If living in an RV is your reward for saving for decades, and you buy your dream RV so you can spend the winters in high-end RV resorts in the Florida Keys, your costs will be higher than most. If you have a fixed income and are looking for ways to make it go further, you can buy a cheap RV and live a more frugal life that is still fun. If your goal is to actually pay off debt, change careers early, or save money for the future, your costs will probably be much lower than they were when you lived the way you usually did.

Your RV lifestyle will probably cost about the same as your current lifestyle because most people like to keep the same level of comfort, amenities, eating out, and other spending habits. Things like groceries and other general living costs will always be a part of your life, no matter where or how you live.

RV Expenses Overview

Here's an outline of some of the typical costs of living in an RV:

RV-SPECIFIC EXPENSES

- Buying an RV (plus tax, loan payments, and interest)

- Insurance

- Service contract extension (optional)

- Maintenance and repairs

- Fuel for driving

- Propane gas to cook, heat, and run the fridge

☐ Campgrounds and parks for RVs

If you buy your RV as a second home, these costs will be on top of the mortgage, rent, and other costs you already have. But if you choose to sell off your house and live in your RV, many of your current home-related costs will go away and be replaced by these.

Your regular living costs will stay the same when you live in an RV. They might look like this:

REGULAR LIVING EXPENSES

☐ Groceries

☐ Entertainment and dining out

☐ Internet and mobile phones

☐ Health care coverage

☐ Personal care (e.g., hair, dental)

☐ Pets (e.g., vetinary visit, food)

☐ Gifts (e.g., birthdays, holidays)

☐ Other luxuries, like treats and other trips or vacations

TO SELL OR NOT TO SELL (YOUR HOUSE)

Now that we've talked about your biggest costs on the road, let's talk about what may be the most important factor in whether or not you can afford to live in an RV full-time: what you plan to do with your regular home. As a homeowner, it can be expensive to take care of your regular home and an RV at the same time. However, if you can trade one for the other, like we did, your finances will get much better very quickly.

How much does your regular life cost you?

You may still be wondering how you're going to pay for everything. Let's look at where your money is going now to see how and where things add up. Here are some common costs that many homeowners face:

- Home mortgage

- Taxes on property

- Utilities (water, electric, gas)

- Fees paid to a homeowners' association (HOA)

- Insurance

- Furniture and decorations

- Upkeep, repair, and modification

- Work in the garden and yard

- Services, like cleaning the house

- You keep buying stuff because you have room for it.

When you look at the fixed costs of owning a home, like the first four items on this list, you'll see how quickly they add up and could be spent on your RV and campgrounds instead. Unless you're remodeling, you rarely need to buy furniture for an RV, and most campground fees cover utility bills (except for monthly stays). With no more property taxes, HOA fees, or yard work, you may be starting to see how RVing could save you money—IF you plan, budget, and buy your RV well. You probably won't need more than one car, so think about how much money that will save you. Don't forget all the "stuff" you won't have to buy anymore!

Making the decision concerning where you currently live

Once you know how much you're spending now, it might be easier to decide what to do. Think about the following.

IF YOU CURRENTLY RENT

If you rent now, the trade-off in terms of money is pretty clear. You just use the money you would have spent on rent and utilities to pay for an RV and camping.

IF YOU WANT TO SELL YOUR HOUSE

If you own a home or have a mortgage on one, the choice is more complicated and unique to you. If you want a new start or a new place to live, you'll probably want to sell your house, maybe with the plan of buying somewhere else later. Selling your home will give you the most freedom because you won't have to worry about taking care of it, even from far away. We found that cutting our permanent ties to the area gave us more mental and emotional freedom as well. Again, this is a very personal choice, and you're the only one who can actually decide what's best for you.

IF YOU WANT TO KEEP—BUT RENT OUT—YOUR HOME

If you want to give yourself a break by taking a "sabbatical" year but love your home and neighborhood, it might be better to rent out your current home (or part of it). You might not want to sell your home right away if you're not sure if you'll like living in an RV and want to try it out for a while. In this case, moving out of your regular home and renting it out can be a good way to make money while you're traveling. There are rental management companies that can take care of the property for you. They charge a fee, but they take care of things so you don't have to worry about much while you travel. Plus, real estate usually (but not always) goes up in value over time, so keeping your home as an asset and renting it out helps make up for the value of your RV going down. Lenders also like people who own their own homes, which could help you get a better interest rate and improve your chances of getting approved for RV financing.

IF YOU WANT TO KEEP YOUR HOME (WITHOUT RENTING IT OUT)

If you have enough money to keep up both a regular house and an RV, you can try out the RV lifestyle more slowly by going on longer trips to see if you like it. This is a great option, especially if your partner or family doesn't like the idea of RVing as much as you do. Some people find it comforting to keep a home base, so that if RVing doesn't work out, they still have the safety of their home to go back to. They might find that they like living in an RV and are ready to give up their home later, but it might be too much to think about all at once. Or, you (or they) might not like it as much as you thought, and your trip might not last as long as you thought. This is something you'll need to talk about and figure out together in order to come up with a plan that works for everyone.

Chapter 9.   RV Checklist

After traveling and living in an RV for years, I know it can be stressful to pack things for a trip. Knowing what to pack can be tricky for a person who is actually new in this world of adventure. However, with time, it gets easier to pack and carry things around while traveling.

As you already know by now, packing all that you want in some limited space can be very challenging. Also, if you carry too much, you may struggle with all the rattling items and the imbalance that the weight may cause. This can be annoying and very dangerous for everybody.

For this reason, it is important to only carry the necessary things that you need. Remember that you will also acquire more things along the way; therefore, you must always leave room for extra stuff that you are likely to pick up.

To assist you in packing and ease you of all the stress, below is a checklist of the very necessary items that you need to carry with you on your trip. This checklist includes essentials, kitchen equipment, groceries, RV accessories, as well as clothing and personal items.

RV Essentials

These are the things that you must carry. These are very necessary for making your life comfortable during the trip.

- ☐ Surge protector
- ☐ Shovel
- ☐ Flashlight
- ☐ Electrical adapters
- ☐ Leveling blocks
- ☐ Electrical and duct tape
- ☐ Water pressure regulator
- ☐ Wheel chocks
- ☐ Battery jumper cables
- ☐ RV-friendly toilet paper
- ☐ Toilet chemicals
- ☐ Extra cotter pins
- ☐ Sewer kit

- Extra motor oil and transmission fluid

- Large bag with zipping for documents like registration, license, and reservations, etc.

- Tire pressure gauge

- Drinking water hose

- Fire extinguisher

- Extension cords

- Emergency road kit

Emergency Items

Safety is a very important thing to consider. No matter where you are going, you could have an emergency that may need some medical attention. In addition, you will have some peace of mind if you know that you have your emergency kit already.

To ensure that you carry everything that you need, write a list of needs that are helpful in case of an emergency. The items in your list could include:

- A fire extinguisher

- Medications

- Smoke detectors

- Carbon monoxide detector

- Fully stocked first aid kit

- ☐ Emergency Hand-Crank / Solar Radio

- ☐ LED Flashlight

- ☐ Hand Warmers

- ☐ Waterproof Matches

- ☐ Emergency Candles

- ☐ Waterproof Poncho

- ☐ Green Lightstick – 12 Hour

Food

So, in your first days, you may not be well conversant with the sort of foods you should carry. You may not know the amount that you must carry. Well, the kind of food and the amount to carry along totally depends on the length of the trip, the place where you are going, and the storage space available.

For instance, you can find RVs with refrigerators as big as the fridges in residential homes. These fridges can hold a large amount of food. When traveling, remember to carry a lot of water, snacks, and food items that you will use when going on your adventures. As for water, do not depend fully on your tank or city water. Rather, carry extra bottles and gallons of water.

Amongst the foods you can carry are:

- ☐ Eggs

- ☐ Vegetables and fruits

- ☐ Drink mix packets

- ☐ Grill meats like burgers and hot dogs

- ☐ Bread

- ☐ Canned foods

- ☐ Butter mixes

- ☐ Condiments, including mayo, mustard, ketchup, etc.

- ☐ Frozen, dried meals

- ☐ Salt

- ☐ Butter or margarine

- ☐ Peanut butter and jelly

- ☐ Cereal

- ☐ Baking items

- ☐ Pepper, spices, and herbs

- ☐ Snacks

- ☐ Cooking oil/ spray

- ☐ Soups

It is important to actually note that some of these ingredients, such as eggs, are things that you can also acquire at any grocery shop in every part of the country.

Household and Kitchen Items

Kitchen items are good because you do not have to actually keep purchasing them every other time during your journey. Knives, pans, and pots last very long. In case you do not have a pressure cooker, it is best to consider getting one. These pots are usually very familiar with RVers because it saves them from buying some other equipment.

If you are a lover of coffee, it would be best not to forget your coffee maker. There is nothing as awesome as sitting outdoors, listening to the sound of the forest, and feeling the breeze while sipping a hot cup of coffee.

So, some of the kitchen items that you could carry include:

- Bowls, plates, and cups

- Water bottles

- Dishtowels

- Garbage bags

- Can opener

- Zip close bags

- Chopping board

- Soapdish

- Potholders

- Skillets

- Plastic wrap

- Utensils/cutting knives

- ☐ Disinfecting wipes

- ☐ Paper towels

- ☐ Napkins

- ☐ Cooler

- ☐ Tongs and skewers

- ☐ Food storage container

- ☐ Camping griddle and pie iron

- ☐ Matches and lighter

Clothing and Bedroom Stuff

This is the trickiest part for most people. This is because a lot of people usually think about the weather and its changes before they set out for the journey.

To handle this menace easily, you can carry clothes that are light and are suitable for any occasion. Some of these clothes are pants that are waterproof, which you can put on a windbreaker or another pair of pants. You can also use them to block the wind and keep you warm. You can also carry one or two thick pairs of socks, along with some firm shoes. Depending on the season, you can also carry a hat to keep you from the sun's rays.

Other things you could carry are:

- ☐ Shoes, including sneakers, hiking boots, sandals, etc.

- ☐ Underwear

- ☐ Sheets and blankets

- ☐ Pillows

- ☐ Clothes hangers

- ☐ Bathing suit

- ☐ Sewing kit

- ☐ Short and long sleeve t-shirt

- ☐ Rain gear

- ☐ Pants and shorts

- ☐ Sweatshirts and jackets

- ☐ Towels

- ☐ Socks

- ☐ Alarm clock

Toys and Gadgets

Toys are fun and healthy at the same time. They bond people together through fun activities. If you are going on a trip with your kids, it would be good to pack these gadgets to keep them from getting bored. You can also pack a few things to keep you occupied when out camping. However, be keen to ensure that you do not overpack.

Some of these things include:

- ☐ Frisbee

- ☐ Books and magazines

- ☐ Hula-hoops, corn hole, horseshoes, etc. for yard games.

- ☐ Playing cards

- ☐ Wood

- ☐ Notepad or journal

- ☐ Fishing gear, plus license, tackle, rods, etc.

- ☐ Guitar

- ☐ Puzzles

- ☐ Camping chairs

- ☐ Hatchet or saw

- ☐ Radio

- ☐ Binoculars

- ☐ Flotation devices

- ☐ Sports equipment, including baseball, basketball, football, etc.

- ☐ Headphones

- ☐ Laptop

Toiletries and Personal Items

These are things that are essential when traveling for a long journey. Most of these are things that you cannot do without. They ensure the comfort of your trip.

These toiletries and personal items are:

- Toothbrush

- Toothpaste

- Batteries

- Medications and prescriptions

- Phone chargers

- Shampoo and conditioner

- Cash and credit cards

- Travel map and campground directory

- First-aid kit

- Contact lenses or glasses

- Reservation confirmations

- Watch

- Lotion

- Sunscreen

- Shaving gel

- Comb and brush

- Bug spray

- Makeup

- Nail clippers

- Floss

- Deodorant

- Razor

- Watch

- Sunglasses

- Hair ties

- Soap

What to Leave Behind

There are actually some things that you can do without on the long RV trip like heavy books. Instead of cramping them up in your RV, you can use the contemporary method of reading ebooks that are readily available online.

In the first year of our trip, my husband Tony, who loves reading, carried so many books, some of which he never got to even read. So, we met a few friends who encouraged us to do away with the old school way of doing things and embrace the new trends. With time, we got used to ebooks and audiobooks found online. Now we have fewer books and more space in our RV.

Other things that you can do without include work out equipment. You may be a lover of fitness and want to continue with your daily work out routines. Well, that may be good, but you will be surprised that once you are on the road, you may never use the equipment. Also, there are so many activities that you will do during camping that will still keep you fit. For example, hiking and swimming can be activities that will help you get enough exercise during the long trip.

Ladies, this may hurt a little, but high-heeled shoes should be left behind. Let's face it; you may never get to use them during your trip. Most of the places that you will go to are not good for high heels; hence they may cause you to break or twist your ankle. For you and your ankles' sake, leave the heels behind.

Documents to Carry

There are documents that you should always have in your RV while traveling around. These documents are essential as they have important information that may be needed in case of an emergency. Now, carrying them does not mean that you are pessimistic and anticipating a problem: however, it is good to always be prepared.

These documents include:

Medical Papers

It is of utmost importance to carry several medical documents with you during your trip. These would be very helpful during an emergency and would help police officers, firefighters, or paramedics help you better and faster. Unfortunately, something fatal may occur, causing you to pass out and not have the ability to speak and express yourself. For this reason, it is actually important that you have your medical records with you to make work easier for those who may want to help you. With the information, they can also manage to help you without giving you medication that could make things worse for you. Please do not assume that things will always be fine. It is good that you be ready.

These documents include hospitalization and surgical histories, health insurance, names and contacts of your current doctor, allergies, prescribed medication that you currently have, as well as any legal records entailing your medical care, such as a power of attorney.

Documents on Insurance

You should always carry insurance information that covers your health and vehicles.

Vehicle-related Documents

These documents include license and information on registration, titles, travel insurance cards, vehicle insurance cards, and information regarding roadside assistance.

For this reason, if you face a problem with regards to your vehicle or, unfortunately, have an accident, this information will be very important to help you get the assistance that you need.

Addresses

When you are away from home, having a copy of people's names and addresses can be very convenient.

While away, you may need to contact one of your neighbors or friends back at home to help you with something important. This could be anything from sorting out some bills or checking your mail; you will need someone to help you with these tasks. For this reason, it is good to have their contacts.

It is good that you have your contacts stored in your smartphone; however, it is very important to also have your friends' email addresses since you may lose signal while out on an adventure.

With the hard copies of contacts and email addresses, you can be sure that you will be able to constantly keep in touch with them and get the information and help that you may need.

Pet Information

If you wish to actually travel with your pet(s), you also need to carry information about it. This is because your pet is very much like you when it comes to some issues to do with health. For this reason, you ought to carry documents like your pet's medical records, list of foods, list of medications, list of allergies, information regarding inoculation, and the family veterinarian's contact information.

While on the road, it is vital that your pet's collar has its identification tags. This will help people contact you easily and help you get your pet back in case it gets lost.

Legal Papers

When going on your trip, you should never forget to carry copies of your legal papers. If you are traveling for an extended time or going full nomad, you should carry copies of your vehicle title, marriage license, military separation papers, divorce papers, health care, and living will documents, passports, deeds, birth certificates, powers of attorney, emergency contacts, as well as the contact information of your attorney.

With this information, you can ensure extra protection in case anything happens to you. You can be surprised how much this information can help when out on the road.

One time, Tony and I had an emergency that needed the attention of our attorney. Luckily, my husband had carried his contact information in his diary, and it saved us a load of work. It would have taken us days to solve the matter, but because we had the information, we got it solved in a few hours.

Therefore, do not ignore the importance of this information. It can save your life!

Information on Tech

To handle your banking and online issues easily while on the road, you will actually need to take with you some papers that hold information regarding the operating system, model, and brand of your computer, passwords, cell phone, virus protection program, and the GPS system. Don't forget to keep a hard copy of the pass

Without this information, it may be challenging to access online services or deal with your technical issues.

Information and Guides About Your RV

Every RV comes with a guide, which provides vast information on handling the RV. This is more like a coaching tool by the manufacturer that will help you deal with arising issues in the RV like mechanical problems. For this reason, it is actually important that you carry these documents with you while traveling around in your RV.

There are also camping guides that are very helpful when traveling around. For instance, The Good Sam Travel and Savings Guide and RVer's Friend have been very helpful to us in the past years as it has provided us with actually a lot of information regarding RV camping. From it, we found campsite locations, RV service shops, as well as information on getting important documents such as fishing licenses. These guides have a lot of information that would be helpful as well as make your RV life more comfortable and fun. They are worth every penny.

Chapter 10.   The Practicality of RVing

Living on the road isn't all fun and games. Unfortunately, there are actually a lot of things that require you to have a permanent address. You must understand how to traverse those things to ensure you can vote, take care of your taxes, and even get your mail.

Voting on the Road

Voting is a big deal for most adult Americans. Everybody knows the importance of getting out of their voting, but that can be tricky for some RVers. How are you supposed to vote in Montana when you have spent the winter in New Mexico?

The good news is, a lot of RVers have been voting while living on the road. You just need to learn what you need to do to make sure your voice is heard.

The first problem that actually comes to mind when it comes to voting and RVing is where do you vote since you don't have a permanent home? How can you get a ballot? In 2004, this permanent house issue became a big topic when some RVers had registered their address in Cleveland, Tennessee, were dropped from the polls. That is where an RV mail forwarding services live. Luckily, this issue has been fixed, and whatever address you have for your "legal house" is going to be the address you use to vote.

For the most part, this is going to be the address you have on your driver's license or the address you use as a mail forwarding service. Remember, voting is a right to all Americans and RVers to vote even though they don't have a brick home. Figure out the jurisdiction you fall under and your house's status to make the rest of the process easier.

Once you have a figured out your legal house's location, you have to get a hold of an absentee ballot. The absentee ballot gives you a way to vote even when you are absent from your jurisdiction. Again, getting an absentee ballot is a right, and nobody can stop you.

There are actually a few different ways to do this. You can call up your local jurisdiction offices, and they should tell you how to get one. If they are dragging their feet, other places can help you. VOTE.org is a website that can help you with all of your voting needs. It gives you guides to absentee voting in all states, helps you register, checks your voter status, regulations, and laws concerning absentee voting, and will survey voter ID laws. That means, if you are having issues getting your hands on a ballot, they can help.

So that you know, do not call your local jurisdiction trying to get an absentee when it's two days before an election. Make sure you actually give yourself plenty of time to request the ballot, get it, fill it out, and return to the proper place. If possible, request your ballot on the day that they are available. You can also check to see if early balloting is available, especially if you are in the area at the time but won't be once actual voting takes place.

Filing Taxes

A lot less fun than voting is doing your taxes every year. For some, all you have to do is enter the info on a W2. For others, things become more complicated, especially if you are like most RVers and run an online business. The good news is, there are an RV tax deduction and credit that you need to make sure you know about, and there are parts of full-time RV living that can get complicated.

First, let's go over the difference between domicile, residence, and tax home. A domicile is a place where you have a mailing address and where your ID is from. This is the address that will be put on the tax return and is likely where you will file your state taxes.

There are often benefits to change the location of your domicile for your travels. For example, a lot of people will choose to domicile in Florida or Texas because those states don't require you to pay state taxes. However, the domicile also affects things like sales taxes on vehicles, insurance costs, and availability, homeschool laws, along with other things. Therefore, you will need to do a bit of research before you make the decision.

The residence is where things get hairy. Your domicile is almost always considered the state of residency, even if you are traveling. That said, there are exceptions. If half of the year or more is spent in a different state, you might have to claim some of the income in that state. You will have to look into this based on your situation.

The tax home is typically used to figure out the mileage deduction for small businesses and refers to the area where you take care of most of your business. For most living in an RV, this becomes your home-on-wheels, which means their tax home travels with them. Wherever your RV is parked is your tax home. That means it typically removes the chance to take a mileage deduction. There are exceptions, but we'll discuss this.

There are work camping tax specifics that you'll need to understand. People will often wonder if they have to claim fringe benefits offered through a work camping position as income. The answer will change whether you file as a small business or employee. If you file as a business, the taxable benefit will be claimed as "bartering." If you are filing as an employee, it should all be rolled into the W2.

There are also non-taxable fringe benefits. These would include educational and healthcare reimbursements. This is because most campers are required to stay onsite, as this is convenient for the employer.

A deduction is an important thing to look at as well. First, RV interest is tax-deductible. If you have a loan on your RV, you can deduct the interest; just make sure you claim your RV as your home.

You will also have business deductions. This can include the internet, equipment you bought specifically for work, and office supplies. However, some business deductions will be different for RVers. First is travel expenses. This is where the tax home comes into play. Since your travel in your tax home, you probably can't deduct your day-to-day travel expenses. After all, you are choosing to travel, and it isn't required.

Then you have the home office deduction. First, do you have space used only as your office and separated from the rest of the home? Since RVs are small, you will likely not have such a space, which means you can't deduct for a home office.

For the first time full-time RVers, it may be a good idea to actually reach out to a tax professional for help. After you have figured things out, you can try handling your taxes on your own.

Getting Mail

Mail tends to be something that we take for granted, but since you won't be living in a stick-built house, getting mail can be tricky. The best part of actually living in an RV is freedom, and nobody wants to be stuck in one place, waiting for their mail to catch up to them. Finding something that is hassle-free and flexible is important.

Your first option could be using friends or family as mail forwarders. However, this typically only works for those who travel for short periods. Also, if you don't get a lot of mail, it could work. In fact, there is a chance you could get your first-class mail forwarded for free. There are issues with this method, though, especially for those who live on the road full-time.

The second would be to use the USPS as the mail forwarder. Mail forwarding, however, is not their forte. This becomes evident if your mail is forwarded to a variety of temporary addresses. They will only forward mail to one location, so this is not a good choice if you relocate frequently.

The third would be to use mailboxes at UPS. However, I wouldn't look too much into them as a full-time RVer because they don't have the types of services you are looking for, and the cost can get up there.

Banking

Banking options are more plentiful than ever, and pretty much all of them are actually going to work as long as they have nationwide access and online services. Still, there are things you have to consider as a full-time RVer. There are different types of banks you can choose from.

First is your traditional bank like Wells Fargo, Bank of America, and Chase. They have the advantage of large nationwide networks of physical branches and ATMs. However, this can be costly, so they often charge monthly account fees depending on what level you choose.

Then you have online banks like Ally and Capital One 360. They typically don't charge any fees and have higher saving rates.

You can also go with a brokerage, as many are offering banking services these days. They are often low-cost and are quite handy if you combine their other services.

Credit unions are also an option. The only thing is you actually have to be a member to join, but they are known for flexibility and great customer service.

Lastly, if you are qualified, you can go with military banks. They often have great reputations, and they have the added advantage of taking care of families who live abroad or travel. These things might not happen, but why risk it?

The big issue has a physical address. Thanks to the Patriot Act, which was passed to protect against terrorist financing and money laundering, all financial institutions have to have verifiable proof of their customers' identities. That includes having a physical address on file. Unfortunately, PO boxes and mail forwarding services are often flagged as "non-residential."

There is an exception in the Patriot Act that allows people who don't have an address to use the address of their next of kin or another contact person. However, banks may not always accept that. While you may not run into any problems, there is a chance that the bank will require you to give them a physical address and prove that you live there. The chances are slim, but having a friend or family member who will actually let you use their address and have a bill sent there is a good idea. The important thing is to make sure that the physical address is in the same state as your domicile.

Dealing with Government Penalties

There is no way around; the government will not reward those living a nomadic life. While they may not actually have set out to screw over the nomads, some laws inadvertently make a nomadic life more challenging. Three main things cause problems.

1. **Can't park on your own property.**

There are plenty of RVers who own land. A home base makes it easier for getting legal documents, voting, and receiving mail. However, not all who own land can live on it in their RV. These are laws that are normally implemented by a city or county council

and aim to keep property values high. Even if a house is built on-site, living in the RV could be considered illegal during that time. This means you need to check local laws before buying a spot of land. But the tricky thing is that these laws can pop up at any moment.

2. **No address means a banking headache.**

We've discussed this a bit already. Once the Patriot Act was made a law, an unseen side effect started to trickle into the community of RVers. When the RVer hits the road, they are leaving behind their address. You have to have an address, though, to have a bank account, and they can deny you if they know that your address is from a mail service. If you already have an actual bank account, you could be all good. However, if you were to create a business, you will likely need to get a business bank account, which will create a real headache.

3.   Voting becomes a pain as well.

We've discussed how to vote, and you shouldn't have issues because voting is a right, but that doesn't mean the state government won't make it a pain. Since many RVers will use a mail forwarding service that will act as their address, that means you will be a resident of a new state, county, and town. Remember that story from 2004 out of Cleveland, Tennessee? In 2018, election supervisor of Clay County, Florida quit accepting new voters who used popular RVers or Cruiser mail forwarding service addresses that originated from St. Brendan's Isle. They also went through 3000 voting roles to get rid of anybody registered through that forwarding service.

Florida is an important voting state, and them doing this could set a precedent. If it seems wrong to you, that's because it is. Their lawmakers want to take away the rights of people living a nomadic life, and they shouldn't be able to do that. Hopefully, this won't become a bigger issue, and Escapees RV Club helped the RVers maintain their right to vote.

Also, absentee ballots can prove a problem. There are some states that require an excuse for obtaining an absentee ballot.

However, it's not all doom and gloom. The good thing about changing your residency when RVing is that you could end up spending less on taxes and vehicle registration fees.

Further Information

The best place to go to gather more information about these struggles would be the Escapees RV Club. They have fought for more rights for those who choose to live life on the road. They are a great resource to have.

Chapter 11.   How to Test Your RV

You absolutely must take any potential RV purchase out for a test run. Don't be alarmed if you are not an expert driver right from the get go. Backing up may be a nightmare—in the beginning. It is a lot like driving a car. Once you actually get the hang of it, it becomes much easier and you won't have to concentrate so hard on the actual driving, backing up or turning corners.

While you are out in the RV, take the time to get a feel for the brakes, adjust the mirrors and turn on the windshield wipers. You need to actually make sure everything is in good working order.

There are many dealerships that will let you "borrow" an RV for a day or two to see if it will suit you and your needs. If this isn't possible, you need to spend an hour at the very minimum going through a motor home and checking out every little nook and cranny. The smallest detail can make all the difference.

When you take a potential purchase out on the road, the following list includes some of the things you want to evaluate on your test drive.

- **Engine idle** — Is it smooth or does it have a hiccup? Does it idle fairly quietly? Note diesel engines (which are common and often better than typical gas engines) are going to be somewhat loud.

- **Braking system** – Class A motor homes have air brakes. You want to make sure the motor home stops appropriately and there isn't any grabbing when the brakes are applied.

- **Acceleration** – Hit the gas and feel the motor home moving forward. Does it cut out or hesitate? Of course the rigs are bigger and are not going to be as fast as your car or truck, but you want the acceleration to be smooth. The motor home should shift gears smoothly without any hitches.

- **Noise** – Listen to the RV as you travel down the highway. Is it louder than you prefer? If so, check out another model. There is a right one out there for you. Listen for any sounds that sound out of the norm for a typical engine. Pinging or grinding noises are a sign of trouble.

- **Cornering** – How does the rig corner? Will you have to make wide turns? If you are going to be driving about town, this could be a problem. You will want to consider scaling down.

☐ **Watch the gauges** – Make sure none creep up while you are driving.

When you get back to the lot, have a second person push on the brakes and use the blinkers while you stand in the back to make sure they work. Do the same for the headlights and any running lights.

Make sure you follow the outline in the above chapter to check out the inside of the RV thoroughly. Open every cupboard and door to get an idea of the space of the RV. Don't assume a cupboard is usable. In many RVs, a cupboard is filled with pipes or tanks and there is no real usable cupboard space for you to store dishes or food.

Chapter 12.   Driving an RV

There are three things you have to keep in mind when you're driving a bigger rig, especially when you're turning: the blind spots, the wide turns, and the rear overhang. Bigger rigs have a longer wheelbase - that's the length between the steer axle or the drive axle - so the turns need to be wider. You have to move further into the intersection before turning; sharp turns near the curb will result in your rear tires climbing over the curb. Blind spots are also bigger; you have to keep an eye on your actual mirrors when you're turning or switching lanes. You also have to actually keep in mind the RV's rear overhang when turning.

The RV's rear overhang starts at the drive axle - also known as the RV's pivot point - to the end of your RV. The sharper the wheel cut or, the sharper you turn, the larger the RV's overhang would swing out towards the opposite direction. If you turn left, the rear will swing right. This doesn't just happen to RVs - it happens on all vehicles, but it's just more pronounced in RVs because they're longer. More often than not, the miscalculation of the RV's overhang swing is the cause of accidents where drivers hit poles, signs, fire hydrants, etc.

It will definitely take some time to get used to, I know. RVs are large, cumbersome beasts for the most part. You'll find that it takes longer for them to accelerate, and they brake slower too. That's why I can't stress this enough: practice makes perfect, and in driving a bigger RV, you'll have to practice a lot to get a sense of how to turn and handle your vehicle easily with hopefully no accidents. Driving a van is highly suggested - start driving with a van or a smaller Class C, especially if you have no prior experience in driving bigger vehicles - and no, your monster truck doesn't count.

That said, here are some driving tips you should know about when you start driving an RV.

Practice

Driving an RV is basically the same as when you've driven any other vehicle - same principles on how to accelerate, how to stop, how to switch gears, etc. - but the size of the RV is such a huge factor that new drivers feel like they're learning to drive all over again when they're in front of the RV's wheel for the first time.

Find yourself an empty parking lot and spend a couple of days in there practicing some rather difficult driving maneuvers. If you've found it difficult to parallel park in your SUV, then you can imagine how hard it would be to park with a big rig. Familiarize yourself with how the rig turns and feels when you're driving it because no one wants to spend their vacation stressed out while driving.

Watch your mirrors all the time. As we said before, the blind spots of your rig are larger than your normal vehicle, so when you look through your mirror, make sure that you will see most of your rig's sides easily. The last thing you want to actually do when you're turning or switching lanes is to crush a mini sedan.

Get a Spotter When You're Packing or Backing Up

Your rearview mirror is going to be pretty much useless, so unless you have a rearview camera mounted at the back of your rig, have someone outside to spot for you to make sure you're not hitting anything. If your rig is especially long, develop hand signals with your partner or get walkie-talkies so you won't be shouting at each other down the length of your RV.

Be Aware of the Weather

You should avoid driving in bad weather. An RV isn't a four-wheel-drive built for running in extreme weather conditions. Besides, the strong winds will make it difficult for you to drive. The RV is a boxy thing - it's not really aerodynamically designed. The wind resistance is only going to slow you down, so when it's raining, snowing, or hailing outside, stop and park somewhere safe first. After all, you have everything you need in your rig - you can camp literally anywhere.

You should make a habit of watching or looking for the weather forecast whenever you're out driving in your RV. It's not always going to be perfect blue skies accompanying you as you go on your epic road trips. That sunny weather has the possibility to take a turn for the worse, so checking the weather app or listening to the weather reports can actually save you a lot of time and effort in the end as well.

It's also more expensive to repair a wrecked RV, so do your wallet a favor and stay put when the weather is bad. You'd also be saving yourself from a lot of potential Walmart overnight stays.

Know Your Rig's Size

Be hyper-aware of the size of your rig - not just the length but also the width and the height. The roads of America are peppered with some low vertical clearance bridges. They just aren't prepared to take on bigger rigs sometimes, so be sure to know where they are and plan your route properly. Most RVs have an average height of 11 to 13 feet, so watch out for those vertical clearance signs - they're there for a reason. It's hard to make a 10-point turn on a narrow road because you can't pass the vertical clearance of a bridge.

Just as important is the rig's width. During road closures, the lanes are narrowed down significantly. There are also some states that limit RVs with widths 8 feet and a half to the interstates, so the bottom line is, if it looks like the RV won't fit, don't push it. You'd only hit something, or worse, you'd get stuck.

So the actual best thing to do is to plan your route in advance. If your RV is especially big, all the more should you stick to your planned route. This way, you won't be surprised by a low clearance bridge or tunnel appearing in front of you. There are tons of apps out there for RV route planning. Some of the good ones may charge a fee, but if you're going to live in an RV, we feel like this is one expense you won't regret paying for.

Drive Slowly

Don't mind the others on the road - they're rushing, and they have smaller cars. Let them honk all they want. Slow and steady wins the race. RV driving experts recommend that when driving an RV, you shouldn't exceed 65 MPH. Not only are you staying safe, but you're also saving gas.

Keep a Safe Distance Between Your RV and the Vehicle in Front of You

An RV is heavy - it's literally a home on wheels. The brakes will not be as fast as they would be on a regular vehicle. It will take time for your RV to roll to a complete stop. You can't and don't want to do sudden stops, else everything inside your drawers will come flying out, or you'll crash into the vehicle in front of you.

Also, you should be wary about riding the brakes of the RV. Riding the brakes may cause it to overheat and malfunction - you don't need me to point out how dangerous that would be if you're going up winding roads or going cross country. Please do your brakes a huge favor - downshift first before breaking.

This is why the safest distance between you and your neighboring driver is around 400 to 500 feet - the more, the better in your case. You would need lots of space in order to brake safely. If someone behind you is rushing and invading your personal space, lengthen the distance between you and the vehicle in front even more. That way, when the one at the back crashes into you, you can avoid crushing the vehicle up front.

Keep Right

Stay on the rightmost lane when driving, especially when you're on the highway. The RV you are driving is big and slow, so stay on the rightmost lane and let the other smaller cars fly past you. Staying on this lane will lessen your anxiety if you're stressed that you're slowing the other cars down - at least I know I do.

Not only will staying in the right lane be the safest for you and for the other cars in the road, but you'll also be nearer to the shoulder so you can easily stop if there's some problem with your rig. And as a bonus, you only have to look at one side mirror: your driver's side mirror.

Now, how about the exits on the highway? If an exit is approaching, switch one lane over and let all the other vehicles go through the exit ramp. After, you can easily switch back to the right lane.

Truck Stops are Your Friend

Normal gas stations are the bane of any new RV drivers: low-hanging roofs and really tight turns. It is a sure recipe for disaster, so when you're new to driving an RV, stick to the truck stops. As the gas pumps in truck stops are built with bigger vehicles in mind, you'd have no problem maneuvering your RV in there.

Get someone to spot for you when you're pulling up while you're at it, just to make sure you're not actually going to hit anything dangerous.

Check Your Engine

Always check and maintain your engine. We've already given you a list of what to pack in case of road emergencies. The most important should be the ones concerning your vehicle safety, so make room for those items. It's also advised to make a checklist and make it a point to inspect your RV before sitting behind the wheel.

- Check all your lights to see if they're working and signaling properly. This includes the RV's headlights, signal lights, and tail lights.

- Check your tires. You should have a portable air compressor with you in your trunk. Check your tire's pressure and tread depth.

- Check your belts and hoses. There shouldn't be any cracks.

- If you are towing something along, check the towing equipment and the hitch, and the safety cables.

- Check for signs of any kind of leaks under your rig

- Check the levels of your oils, brake fluid, transmission, and coolant and top them if needed.

☐ Check your brakes. This includes the air brake, parking brake, and - if you're dragging a towable - also check your tow brakes.

Check Other Systems

And lastly, before you drive off into the sunset after checking your engines, you should also check all the other parts of your RV before you actually make your way out of the parking lot or campsite. An RV has a lot of miscellaneous things attached to it, like steps, awnings, etc. So you should:

Make sure your smoke and gas detectors are all in working order.

Check to see if your propane tank has any leaks.

Retract everything you pulled out when you camped and lock them, so they're ready for travel. This includes awnings, steps, jacks, slide-outs, wheel blocks, etc.

Don't forget everything you placed outside when you camped. This may include your tables, chairs, pets, and other camping gear you placed outside.

If you're in a campsite with partial or full hookups, disconnect from all hookups: electrical, water, sewer, cable tv, etc.

Make sure your stove, heaters, and burners are off or anything that's powered by your propane tank.

All windows and doors should be latched. You don't want them torn off when you're on the interstate.

Check if your ladder is stowed properly.

Check your roof. Close all your vents; stow your antenna and satellites.

Close all your drawers, cabinets, and doors securely.

Switch off any electrical appliance that's connected to your 12V battery. You don't want to run out of electricity in the middle of your trip.

Check your water tanks. Fill up your freshwater tank if needed; empty your grey and black water tank as needed.

Chapter 13.   Making Your RV Feel Like Home

Home is where the heart is, even if said home is moving around a lot.

People often wonder if they can make their RV feel a little more like the home they've left behind. It is definitely possible, and I am going to show you how.

Home Tip #1: Change the RV Mattress

The mattress that comes with your RV might not be suitable for you, so make sure you change it to something a bit more comfortable. If you feel that getting a brand-new mattress is not something you would like to invest in, there are cheaper alternatives. For one, you can get a mattress topper, which is essentially a layer of bedding you add on top of your mattress. Alternatively, you could even take the mattress from your home and put it in your RV if the mattress can fit on the RV's bed.

Home Tip #2: Add Wall Decor

Include pictures, stickers, or other wall decorations to bring a little color and life to your RV. Adding wall clocks showing times from different parts of the world is also a wonderful addition.

Here are some other ideas you can consider:

- A map of the country or region

- Photo frames containing fun sayings or messages

- Hanging pots and plants (make sure they are completely secure, or you could choose artificial plants, as well). HINT: You can choose to take down the pots and plants when you are traveling and set them up again after you have parked your RV, but that means you have to manage your space very well since these decorative items can actually take up a lot of space.

- LED lights

- Flameless candles (they set the ambience without setting your RV on fire)

- Hanging wicker baskets is a great idea for décor and storage

Home Tip #3: Use Oil Diffuser

Get your RV smelling fresh. It doesn't take too long for the RV to accumulate a plethora of scents from your travels. Using an oil diffuser can make all the difference in the world. Scents such as eucalyptus add a little freshness into the air, while rose can provide a wonderful sweet smell. Look at different oils and find the one that suits you. If you are traveling with other people, let them smell the scents before you buy them so you can actually find out if anyone is allergic to the fragrance.

Home Tip #4: Home Comforts

Remember how we talked about bringing bathroom slippers and cutlery? Many people prefer to buy new items for the RV, but I like to have things from my home because they make the RV feel lived in. Bring in your favorite coffee mug. Get your comfortable home slippers. Add your welcome mats, if you would like. Things you have already used before entering your RV have a sense of value to them, and bringing them to your RV transfers that value to your motorhome.

Home Tip #5: Add Curtains

If your RV comes with valences, then see if you can replace them with curtains. With such a simple addition, the interior of your RV transforms into something comfortable and cozy.

Home Tip #6: Bring Your Favorite Tunes

I am serious. Playing your favorite music in the RV can actually make a whole lot of difference.

Let me give you an example.

If you had a particular playlist you used to play while working from home, then playing that playlist in your RV can actually make you feel like you are once again working from home.

But there are other situations where music could very well be the remedy. You are going to face some challenges while RVing—perhaps it could begin to rain heavily and you might have to stop for a while until the weather changes for the better. You are unable to do anything but sit and wait out the downpour. During those times, think about the moments when you used to play your favorite songs at home, the ones you or your entire family would enjoy. Perhaps you and your family used to take turns playing music because one person could not decide whose music was better until, eventually, everyone decided they should each have a turn at picking a track.

Recreate the same experience in your RV. Either put on a nice playlist or let people take turns playing some of their favorite songs.

Allow for this experience to happen not just during a chaotic situation, but for other times as well. Enjoy your favorite music and the preferred music of your passengers whenever they are in the mood, just like you would at home.

Home Tip #7: The Great Outdoors

Just because you have an RV does not mean you cannot extend your home space to the great outdoors. In fact, that is one of the benefits of having such a vehicle. You can have so many unique outdoor vistas, locations, and sights to experience.

To do this, see if you have enough space to pack an outdoor tent. In fact, if you are staying at a particular spot for a few days, you can even use the tent as an extension of your living space. Toss in a mat and a few cushions and you could work, relax, or just have fun outside.

Home Tip #8: Keep Things Neat and Organized

I've already made a point about this, but it requires mentioning again because this time, it concerns the environment you are trying to maintain. Clutter not only disrupts the homey atmosphere you are trying to establish, but also has an impact on your mind. More clutter makes your space feel untidy and creates a sense of chaos, subconsciously creating a sense of chaos in your mind as well.

Have you actually ever been in the middle of a traffic jam and felt the stress it gives you? Now think back to those times you were in the presence of nature, where there were not a lot of people around and you felt peaceful and serene.

The same situation applies here. When you are in the presence of cutter and chaos, your mind reacts to it accordingly. If there is a sense of order and tidiness, however, your mind itself begins to project order and tidiness into your life.

With the above tips, you have made a wonderful transition to your RV lifestyle, but transitioning is only the first step. Now you have to start living in your RV and take care of it.

Chapter 14.   Setting-Up at the Campsite

Level - Side-to-side

One of the actual most important things is to level the RV when you first arrive at the campsite before you start hooking-up or setting-up. Whether you have a towable RV or a drivable RV, the same principles apply. Position the RV on the campsite exactly where you want it to be. Go to the side of your RV and place the level against the side of the RV in an up and down position, just like your body standing. Try to place the level directly above the tires, but if that puts you on a slide out, then move forward or backwards just far enough to get to the actual side of the RV. Determine if you are level, and if not, to which side is the RV leaning?

In time you will learn to figure out how much leveling is needed by the reading on the level, but to begin with, it is trial and error. Lay the fence board beside the tires on the low side of the RV. Pull the RV forward just until the rear tire is clear of the board. Slide the board in the path where the tire(s) just was/were, then back the RV onto the board. If that is not enough leveling, then you may need to use the leveling blocks (thicker than the deck board) which can be put together like legos in a stair step type pattern to make it possible to back onto them.

Wheel chocks

Once you are level, CHOCK YOUR WHEELS!

If you are on fairly level ground, I recommend placing a wheel chock in front of the front tire on each side, and behind the rear tire on each side. If you have a single axle, place a wheel chock on each side of the tire on each side.

If you are parked on an incline, put the wheel chocks in front of or behind each tire, depending on which way is downhill and the direction the RV may roll.

Level - Front-to-rear

If you have a towable RV, it is time to disconnect. If you have a drivable RV, there is nothing to disconnect unless you are towing a vehicle. Regardless of the surface type, it is always good to put the 2" x 10" pressure treated blocks down for your landing gear feet to land on (or your leveling blocks if using them instead of lumber). If you have an auto-leveling system, you know what to do now. If you have manual leveling jacks, usually the front landing gear is what you use to level front to rear (with the level on the floor inside the RV or on the kitchen counter). The manual rear landing gear on most RVs is not designed to lift the RV to a level position, it is there to add support once you are level.

Electrical connection

Some RVs have the shore power cable already wired in on one end with a plug on the other end. Some shore power cables have a twist-lock type connector to plug into the side of the RV and a plug on the other end. If you have the twist-lock, I recommend plugging into the RV first. Next go to the power post and make sure all of the circuit breakers are turned off. If you have a surge protector, plug the shore power cable into it first, then plug the surge protector into the power post and turn the breaker on that corresponds with your RV's power setup (usually 30 amp or 50 amp). If you do not actually have a surge protector, plug the shore power cable into the power post BEFORE turning on the appropriate circuit breaker. If you have a surge protector, some of them wait about 2 minutes before turning on the power to the RV, so if the display is lit up, but you do not have power in the RV, wait 2-3 minutes and it should turn on or have an error on the display.

City water connection

Some city water connections have the fitting where your drinking water rated hose will screw on coming straight out the side, and others have it where the hose is hanging from the spigot. If it has your hose coming straight out the side, I would recommend using one of your 90 degree water hose elbows to take the crimping pressure off of the hose. The same thing applies when connecting the water hose to your RV, you may need a second 90 degree hose elbow.

I used to put my water pressure regulator on the RV end of the hose until one day we were sitting outside at a campsite and I looked over and noticed the water hose was blown-up to almost twice its normal size.Now I put it on the spigot end of the hose. Once firmly connected to the spigot and the RV. Go inside and turn water fixtures OFF before opening the spigot. As you turn the water on at the spigot, I recommend going slowly. Once you hear the air noise stop, you should be safe to turn it fully on. Go inside and slowly open the cold water valve on a sink or shower and let the air bleed out until you have a steady flow of water. Next do the same with the hot water valve. If your hot water tank has been drained, it may take much longer for water to come from the hot tap than it did for the cold as the hot water tank is filling up.

Hot water tank

Be completely sure you have water in your water heater before you turn it on. If your RV has been winterized, make sure the correct valves are open for city water connection. If you have someone winterize the RV for you, make sure they show you (and you take notes) exactly what steps to take to connect to city water correctly after the winterization.

Sewer hose

If you are actually at a campsite that has a sewer connection, you can go ahead and hookup to your sewer connection. Make sure your sewer hose is well attached to the output line from your RV. Run the 90 degree end of the sewer hose to the campground sewer connection and secure the sewer hose to the connector. Some are threaded and you can screw your 90 elbow into the connector. If so, I recommend not screwing it in very much or you may have great difficulty trying to disconnect. If it is not one you can screw into, try to find a rock, piece of firewood, or something that will help hold the hose connector firmly in the sewer connection. When you pull the handle and liquid starts running through the hose, you want to be 100% sure it is going onto the sewer, not on the ground.

Drain valves

You will likely have 2 drain valves fairly near the sewer connection on the RV. One should be labeled Black, and the other Gray. We happen to have 2 gray tanks on our 5th wheel, so we have a third handle labeled "galley". Black water is strictly from the toilet. Gray water comes from the shower and the sinks.

You likely have some type of tank monitor panel in the RV somewhere. You will probably see a button for "battery", "fresh", "black", and "gray". There are sensors in the tanks that are supposed to tell you the current level of liquid in the tanks. The sensors are notoriously inaccurate, especially the black tank as toilet paper or other solids may catch on the sensor and show a reading even when the tank is full. I have discovered that although the mid-level readings may not be accurate, usually when it shows "full", that is most often correct. You want to keep the drain valves CLOSED during normal operation, especially for the black tank. With the black tank, if you were to leave the valve open, as you flush the toilet, the solids will land in the tank and the liquid drains out, and over time you have the equivalent of a concrete mountain in your tank. Leaving the black valve closed until ready to drain the tank allows the liquid to remain in the tank and help break-down the solids. I like to have plenty of water in the gray water tanks, so when I am finished draining the black tank, I have relatively cleaner water to run through the sewer hose next to help clean it out and remove most of the odor.

If you are at a campground that does not offer sewer hookups at the sites, there will most likely be a dump station near the exit of the park. It would be unreasonable to completely disconnect the RV to go to the dump station, then have to come back and re-level and re-hook everything. A portable rolling waste tank is handy in these cases. You can drain your tank(s) into the portable waste tank, and most have a handle that will connect to your trailer hitch and you tow it to the dump station to empty it.

Tank chemicals

I have always used holding tank chemicals for the black tank to help break-down solid waste (another reason to have liquid in the black tank). You can find different brands and types online, or locally in the camping section at your big box stores. Most common are small bottles, often sold as an 8 pack, or pods that look like laundry or dishwasher pods. Some people also use a gray water tank deodorizer, usually sold as a liquid in a large bottle in the same place you find the black tank treatment.

Chapter 15.   RV Camping Benefits

A little about me: I've been living out RVs and campers for seven years. This has allowed me to have many fun experiences that other people wouldn't. I started off on this journey as a single man in his thirties, traveling around the USA. Since that time I have become married, and my wife now enjoys the RV lifestyle as well.

There are a lot of reasons why living out of an RV might appeal to you. Let's go over some of them first:

☐   **It's Cheap**

Whether you paid off your RV completely or you are on a payment plan, it's still going to be a lot cheaper than owning a house / mortgage. You do have to think about costs like gas and maintenance (and payments if you haven't purchased your RV completely). If you do a lot of travel, these costs can add up. But it usually won't exceed $700 or $800 per month.

☐ **It's Even Cheaper if You Want**

If you are low on money, you can choose to live an extra budgeted RV lifestyle. What this means is you find your perfect geographic area (maybe it's beautiful coastal California) and you move between different parks, or boondocking (more on this later) without traveling too far. By accumulating less miles, you spend less gas, and you take fewer trips to the repair shop. Including food you can live on less than $500 a month this way, no joke! I think this is a good option if you are very low on money. But you don't want to live like this forever (you should be working some type of a job still and making money even if you are living on the road!).

☐ **You Feel Free**

You don't have to be stuck any one place. You can simply move to the next spot any time that you are not satisfied somewhere. If you don't like the weather, the people or anything else, just turn the engine on and go elsewhere!

☐ **You Reconnect with Nature**

Nothing really beats the feeling of being in a nice park, waking up and cooking on your grill outside, and / or drinking filtered water directly from the creek!

☐ You Learn to Cook

Your RV will have a gas stove. You can stock up and cook for yourself a lot. You will start to feel very self-sufficient after a while.

☐ You Can Meet People

I don't believe in being a hermit. The RV camping community means wherever you go to park at, you'll meet neighbors. So, make it a point to meet up with them, chat, hike, hang out. If you don't like someone, well you don't have to stay their neighbor! Just move somewhere else. But hopefully you'll encounter far more friendly people who you want to actually stay in touch with than not.

☐ You Can Visit Friends and Family Easy

No more having to stay at pricy hotels or burden friends and family by staying on their couches. Instead, you are always self-sufficient.

☐ You Become a Minimalist

Our lives are filled with too much junk. What I found in my 20s was that everyone all over the place was working really hard to get new TVs, home furnishings, and more bull#%# thinking it would make them happier. I knew a woman when I lived in NYC who spent $2,000 on a feng shui expert for her apartment for crying out loud. That's money you could instead spend on seeing beautiful new locations. Living like this, you appreciate where you put your money and understand where real value is.

☐ You Complete Your Bucket List

Many people don't even travel until they're already retired. A big waste. This way, you can start enjoying life and seeing cool places right away.

So, are you feeling excited yet? Good! These are all good reasons to become a camper. Now, keep in mind there are some downsides, too. If you really want the security that comes with living and working in one place, you might not like this type of lifestyle so much. Also, you need to love the road, driving, and travel. You have to be good at adapting to new situations and being relaxed when things go wrong. If these attributes are good for you, then it's time to get started.

Chapter 16.   RV Camping and Driving Tips That Will Make Your Travel Easy

Map Your RV Travel Location

First thing that you actually need to do is that map RV travel destinations properly. Keep the map of the place where you want to go in your RV. The advantage of RV is that you can place it anywhere but getting the proper plan is so crucial. Because in this way you will not lose the way. Moreover keep some interesting sites in your mind before driving your RV. The sites will allow you make your travel and stay amazing. If you have already decided about the places where you want RV camping then its really good. But still you need to have a map and learn about the tracks and roads.

If you are not sure about RV camping sites then you can contact with tourism boards. Besides you can use some media such as internet for getting the proper guide about sites. You also need to bring a right GPS system with you especially at the time when you are a beginner or newer to RV travel. If there are some easier routes then choose those instead of putting yourself in huge difficulty.

Check for Important Things

You also need to check for some important things for your RV camping. Get a checklist of all those things that you think are important for RV camping. For instance you need to check and locate all important campground connections. Besides you also need to make sure that your recreational vehicle is level. Next to it also check for electric systems, gas and water hook ups. These things are important to check for surviving and successful RV camping.

Make your RV camping comfortable one. You can do it in so many amazing ways. Keep DVDs and some latest or CDs with you. Moreover lawn chairs are also good to carry as they also provide comfort. When you leave for your home then still there is a need to check for all such things, don't forget that.

Prepare First Aid Kit

In the previous chapter you learned about some safety tools and equipment that are crucial to carry in your RV. First aid kit is one of the mentioned safety tools. Make sure that you have stocked your first aid kid with all the necessary things. You can also keep it in outside storage compartment. Your RV kit may include ointment, insect repellent, bandages, scissors, over the counter pain reliever, an emergency supply of must have medication and so on.

Moreover you can also make an extra kit for your RV. You can make it by adding extra batteries, pens, paper, flashlight, disposable camera, charger, radio and cell phone. In your RV you are also required to put the contact information. For instance you can include information about insurance agents, doctors and family members.

RV Camping and Your Kids and Pets

If you have decided to bring your children with you for RV camping then its really a great idea. You can bring them with you as they will also enjoy visiting some new place. They will also learn about different culture and people. RV camping will be equally amazing for your children as well.

When you take your children for RV travel make sure that they have enough space in the RV. If they have some toys and want to play then give them their time and space. Because in this way they will learn and enjoy more. Besides during your RV camping take your children for some outdoor activities. In this way they will enjoy RV trip with you.

Moreover if you have some pets and want to take them with you for RV camping then still it's really a great idea. But remember here that not all the parks allow the pets in RV camps. So before thinking about the pets make sure that you have got permission from the authorities.

Next to it when you enter or leave your RV camp tell your children about it. Tell them how to keep the personal stuff, how to arrange the things, how to stay connected and how to navigate properly from RV camps.

Get Help from Your Friends

During your RV travel if you find any difficulty then you can ask other RVers. They will absolutely come to help you. Usually beginner RVers face a lot of problems during their first travel. Though they have all the necessary things that they must have such as map and communication devices but still odds are always there.

No matter how intensive search you have made and how much you read about the place but while coming on the road you can face some issues that you never imagined. So prepare yourself for everything. Moreover it might happen that you ignored most of the things during your RV travel such as storage places and so on. In all such cases you can get help of some other RVers.

It's not like that all the RVers with whom you are going to travel are good. Besides it's also not compulsory that all of them will become your fast friends. But it's good to be good with all the RVers and they will assist you like your best friends.

Tow Vehicle

Most of the people consider the fuel economy in mind when they think of purchasing the vehicle. This fact then further lead to towing their recreational vehicle/trailer. Whenever you prepare or get your trailer make sure that it is well within rating limitations of the desired tow vehicle. This has so many advantages such as it will have effect on how the combinations stops, accelerates and handles.

Pulling a Trailer

In most of the RVs electric trailer brakes are used and operating such brakes is difficult as well. Such electric brakes highly differ from the hydraulic brakes that are present in your tow vehicle. The eclectic brakes work on a different principle and work until you hold your foot on the brake pedal. So learning about the electrical brake system is so crucial for the beginners when you leave your home for RV camping.

Towing Guidelines

Another concern might be to handle your trailer at highway speeds. This is also important to learn and mange. You can overcome this problem in so many ways. First of you can focus on the construction of your RV. Use a lightweight construction techniques so that later on towing become easier.

Moreover there is also a need to show concern about the size of recreational vehicle. Small and large sizes of such vehicles have their own advantages and disadvantages. In case the approximate size of your trailer will be large then it will be more exposed to passing traffic and wind. In this way such things will greatly affect the stability of Recreational Vehicle. Besides poor loading techniques can also prove a great hindrance while travelling.

Proper Weight Distribution

Balancing is another important factor that you must consider before driving your recreational vehicle. Too much loaded RV is not good because later on it cause some balancing problems. On the other hand the second thing that is important in this regard is that there should be proper weight distribution. If you have loaded somewhat good enough material in your RV but its not organized or arranged in a proper way then still it will cause balancing problems while towing.

If you have overloaded your RV then at the time of towing the towing vehicle will lose the control and move back and forth on the road. Some people have mentioned their bad experiences regarding towing vehicles. They say that they feel several problems especially on the highway roads when the RV is overloaded. They can't balance it and the chances of accidents become more.

Some Other Towing Tips

First of all towing will add a great experience to your driving. Moreover there are also some other advantages of learning towing the vehicle on the road. If you are towing RV vehicle then try to be slower even on the highway roads. The reason is that you will not face swaying and balance problems. A slow speed will allow you to reduce stress. Hence in this way you will be more comfortable at them time of towing your Recreational Vehicle. Moreover you are also required to give a lot of time to yourself on the road so that you may take an appropriate action at the spot.

In short, these are some of the RV camping and driving tips that can help you for towing your vehicle and staying in a good way in your RV camp area.

Chapter 17.   How RVers Save Money on Food, Gas, Camping, and Maintenance

If you like to go shopping, buy new clothes, buy the latest gadgets, go to concerts and sporting events, like new cars, want the latest cell phone, and like to eat out all the time, you're going to end up spending as much (and maybe even more) money living in an RV as you're spending now because. . .

Moving into an RV won't change who you are.

You have to make a conscious effort to change your ways. One of the first things you actually have to do to RV on a dime and a dream is to find ways to live and not spend so many dimes.

How RVers Save Money

Your best option to save money is to make changes to areas where most of your money is being spent. You can't save any money by cutting back on how much you spend on salt because if you totally eliminated salt, it wouldn't save enough to matter.

I know, I'm being facetious, but I'm doing it to make a point. It reminds me of the mother who said to her kid, "If I've told you once, I've told you a million times. Don't exaggerate."

I got off track. Let's get back to how RVers save money.

To save money, you have to cut back in the areas where you're spending a lot of money. Keep detailed records of every penny you spend for a month or so and you might be surprised at the areas where you're spending money. Armed with this information, you can make some informed decisions about where and how to cut back on your spending.

When you're RVing, here are the areas you need to look at closely

☐ **Eating out:** First, don't eat out very often. Make it a special occasion. If you eat out a lot, then it's no longer a special occasion. Also, skip the chain restaurants and the tourist places. Eat at the local mom and pop places and you will get to experience the real cuisine of the area.

☐ **Don't waste food:** Even if you eat most of your meals at home, you may still be wasting a lot of money by throwing away too much food. One way to save a lot on food is to start planning every meal by looking in the refrigerator and seeing what leftovers you have and then thinking what you would need to add to those leftovers to make a good meal. We're all guilty of leaving leftovers in the back of the refrigerator too long and then throwing them out. And we all know ways to save when buying food. We just don't do it. Cut out junk food, shop at discount stores like Aldi, and buy mostly real food—beans, rice, veggies—cut back on protein and high-priced cuts of meat. Also, watch fruits and veggies closely and be sure to eat them before they actually go bad.

☐ **Gas (or diesel fuel):** The best way to save money on gas is not to travel as much. Stay in one place for a month or more and enjoy getting to know the area. Also, you can save on gas by going slower. I've found that I get a lot better gas mileage driving at 55 mph than I do at 65. And if I bump it up to 70, my mileage really goes down.

☐ **Campground fees:** You can save a lot on campground fees by a doing a lot of boondocking (which actually means camping for free on public land). Some RVers do this almost exclusively. You can also save a lot by staying at campgrounds for a month or more at a time. The monthly rate at most campgrounds is about twice the weekly rate. Many campgrounds have workcamper programs where you can work about 20 hours a week and camp for free. You can join PassPortAmerica.com and camp at over 2,000 campgrounds for half price. There are some restrictions, like in most campgrounds you can only stay for one to three nights and sometimes you can't stay on weekends, but these restrictions are sometimes negotiable. Also, when you're on the road and want to stop for the night, don't pay top dollar to stay at a campground for one night. Stay at a Walmart for free. I do it all the time.

☐ **RV maintenance:** The Camping World service center near where I'm camping recently raised their hourly rate from $129 an hour to $142 an hour. I use them for some things, but you can save a lot by doing as much of your RV maintenance work yourself as possible. You can learn how to fix a lot of problems by watching YouTube videos. Just describe your problem and you might be amazed at how many videos show up. And, of course, do a lot of preventive maintenance work on your RV. Another way I handle maintenance work is by using a mobile RV tech. He is less expensive, and I get to watch how he fixes something. That way, the next time (and there will be a next time) I can fix it myself. I have also found a reliable truck repair place that charges about 1/3 of what the RV shops charge. The owner of the shop used to have a Class A RV and knows how to repair most things on an RV.

If you could get these five categories down to zero, the RVing lifestyle wouldn't be expensive at all. Of course, you can't get them down to zero, but for most people, these expenses can be cut way down and without any decrease in the quality of life or enjoyment—just follow the advice I've outlined.

One other point—don't be a tourist. One of the best ways RVers have found to save money is to stop being a tourist. Many new RVers spend a lot of money when they first start RVing because they act like they're on vacation and do things as though they are a tourist, eating out a lot, spending money on tourist attractions, and just generally acting like they're on vacation.

Remember that you're not on a full-time vacation and you're not a tourist. If you do all of the tourist things, you're going to blow your budget in a hurry. I've had several RVers tell me that they spent a lot more money the first year they were on the road than they do now. They say that it's more fun to be a temporary resident in an area than it is to be a tourist, and, of course, a lot less expensive.

Save and Splurge

One advantage of saving a lot of money is that it gives you more money to spend on things that really make you happy. You can do a few tourist things, and buy a few gadgets, but only a few.

I don't spend much on clothes and I don't eat out a lot. (I do like to go out and have a glass of wine and listen to live music from time to time.) Another area where I have to watch my budget is that I like gadgets, especially things for the motorhome.

Here are some of the gadgets I've spent money on over the last year: a five-stage battery charger, two more 6-volt coach batteries, a battery monitoring system, external sensors for the holding tanks so I can get accurate readings of the levels, a new ham radio antenna, a quad-copter to hopefully make my YouTube videos more interesting, and the list goes on.

None of these items were things I had to have. They were just things I wanted. I think you can see how buying gadgets could get out of hand and blow a budget. I have to watch myself (and my budget) because I love gadgets.

Chapter 18.   What to Know, and Where to Go

In this brief chapter, you will learn about Choosing a Destination and How to Get There.

Choosing a Destination

RVParky: This app is an RV park directory written by an RVer with user-generated reviews, images, and information. It works with GPS and displays RV parks, campgrounds, and RV-friendly stores on a clickable map, and it works equally well on mobile devices or computers.

Free Camping: This is an RV community-driven app and website that helps you find user-reviewed free camping sites of all types on a clickable map, then uses its built-in trip planner to map your trip. You can also filter results by amenities desired. Free Camping is free; however, you will need to create an account to get the most benefit from it.

Reserve America: Reserve America is a free membership-based app and website. It is unique in that you can search for, find, and reserve a spot within the app including hiking trips, day-use facilities, lodging, and other outdoor activities like fishing trips. It is one-stop shopping.

RVLife: A subscription mobile device app that helps you find a campground, fine-tune it with multiple levels of clickable amenities, read the reviews, and map the trip from within the app. A unique attribute of this app is the downloadable map for when you are out of the range of cell towers.

Recreation.gov: Federal facility directory website and app that draws from 12 federal agencies such as the National Forest Service, National Park Service and Bureau of Land Management. This resource also has a trip builder that helps you to search for a site across 3,500 federal facilities.

How to Get There

RV Trip Wizard: Find campgrounds, points of interest, determine cost and set driving times and distances with this web-based application. This application is different in several ways from other trip planers. First, Whereas RV trip planners tend to show only the campgrounds affiliated with their respective publishers, RVTW shows all campgrounds. Second, it uses a map interface to set driving time and distance via concentric user-determined circles. You determine how large the circles are based upon your endurance. Third, it has cost monitoring features built in that allow you to factor tolls, fuel, campgrounds, food and other costs to watch the overall trip cost.

Copilot: This is a highly-recommended, version-specific navigation and traffic app for either cars, trucks or RVs that requires an annual $29.95 membership. The app looks like a conventional GPS unit, and allows for out-of-cell tower use via downloadable offline maps that work with the GPS chip in your device.

While You Are Traveling

GPS units: Many RVers prefer to use a separate GPS device for their travels. There are many from which to use, and RVers tend to choose the RV-specific units that provide live-traffic capability. The benefit of using stand-alone GPS units is they usually have much larger screens that are not obscured by sunlight, they do not tie up your smart device, nor are they dependent upon either cell tower service or downloadable maps that can clog up your device. Expect to pay upwards of $300 for premium units such as the Garmin RV 770 LMT-S or the Rand McNally RVND 7730 LM.

Map: The Rand McNally Motor Carrier's Atlas is the RVers best off-line friend. It is the same atlas commercial trucker drivers use, and it is extremely helpful in showing roads with weight, height, axle, and length limitations. Expect to pay around $20 for this atlas in softcover format, or around $75 for laminated, spiral-bound versions. The benefit of using this is to "sanity-check" your GPS, to see the entire route at once, to enable less-stressful on-the-fly travel planning.

iExit: This is a free, web-based and mobile device application that watches your location on the highway and displays upcoming gas, food, shelter and rest stops by highway exit number. When you click on an exit, the app lists its services including the price of fuel. It connects to other apps such as Yelp and Google Maps, so you can click to review or click to get directions. You can either discover and map the stops ahead of time or find yourself on the map via your mobile device's location services. If you are going to keep an app going while on the road, this is the one.

Rest Stops: This app enables you to find a rest stop by drilling down by state, highway, and direction of travel. Once found, you can get directions with Waze, Google Maps, or Apple Maps from within the app. The app also shows RV dump stations.

Sidebar: Temporary/Overnight Stops

Big Box Overnighting: Call ahead, introduce yourself to the manager if you can, buy something while you are there, do not run your generator or kick out your slides, pick up after yourself, and park out of the way. The most common stops are Wal-Mart, CostCo, Sam's, Cabela's, Camping World, Cracker Barrel, and truck stops.

Chapter 19.   Operating and Maintaining Your RV

Focus: Learn Beginner Basics For Operating And Handling An RV.

Easily, one of the most daunting parts of hitting the road in an RV is learning how to operate and maintain the RV correctly. Even though the process is stressful, it is all about practicing and mastering the right rules for your RV. In this chapter, you will learn beginner basics for operating and handling your RV. Take a look.

Tools You Will Need for RV Operation and Traveling

The first step to operating and maintaining your RV is to get everything you need for a safe trip. There are some tools you will need to keep in your RV at all times. These tools will ensure that you have a safe and enjoyable ride. Here is a list of tools you need to pack in your RV whenever you go out on the road, even for a quick trip:

- ☐ Air compressor
- ☐ Bottle jack
- ☐ Bubble level
- ☐ Drill and drill bits
- ☐ Duct tape
- ☐ Flashlight/headlamp
- ☐ Folding tree saw
- ☐ Hammer
- ☐ Knife
- ☐ Leather work gloves
- ☐ Multi-bit screwdriver
- ☐ Multi-purpose adhesive
- ☐ Multi-tool
- ☐ Pliers
- ☐ Socket and ratchet set
- ☐ Spare parts
- ☐ Spray lubricant
- ☐ Super glue
- ☐ Tape measure
- ☐ Tire pressure gauge

- ☐ Two-way radios

- ☐ Utility knife

- ☐ Vinyl adhesive

- ☐ Wire cutters

- ☐ Zip ties

- ☐ Spare Fuses

Once you have gathered all of these tools, make sure to place them in a safe and easily accessible place. You will want to be able to access these tools at a moment's notice. So, put them someplace obvious. Additionally, be sure to recheck these tools every year so you can replace broken items and refill the bag. That way, you always have these tools ready to go from year to year.

Tools You Will Need for Camping

In addition to the actual items above, you will want some additional tools for camping. These camping tools will ensure you have everything you need whenever you have a planned camping trip. These tools will also come in handy in emergency scenarios when you have to camp out roadside. Here is what to pack:

- ☐ Axe

- ☐ Bungee cords

- ☐ Compass

- ☐ Extra water

- [ ] First-aid kit

- [ ] Glow sticks

- [ ] Hand-held emergency generator

- [ ] Heavy-duty flashlight

- [ ] Lanterns

- [ ] Maps

- [ ] Matches

- [ ] Ropes

- [ ] Survivalist handbook

- [ ] Tarps

- [ ] Tent

- [ ] Tent repair kit

Between the list of RV tools above and this list of camping tools, you will have everything for an emergency situation, whether you just need to fix up your RV or you need to actually spend the night in the wild.

Practice Your RV Driving Before Hitting the Road

For many first-time RVers, the most stressful part of hitting the road is driving a large vehicle. If you have never driven a vehicle as large as an RV before, you will likely run into a lot of stress and difficulties. To ensure that your trip is super safe and fun, it is important to practice your driving before you actually hit the road. By practicing your driving beforehand, the only thing you have to worry about is getting to your destination on time. It is important not to go on your travels until you are comfortable driving your RV.

While you are learning how to drive your RV, there are some things you want to watch out for. Here are some tips to ensure you are driving your RV safely:

- Know the height and width of your rig so you do not get into tight-fitting situations.

- Always monitor your speed. You should generally avoid traveling over 65 mph since these vehicles are so large and heavy. Get the feel of how fast your RV feels while you are driving.

- Stay out of the far left lane. Since you will likely be going underneath the speed limit, avoid the fast lane. Instead, try to drive in the lane furthest to the right.

- Maintain a safe distance from the vehicles in front of you. Because RVs are so large, they require more braking distance. Stay about 400 to an actual 500 feet behind the driver in front of you, so you have enough room to brake safely.

- Pay attention to the weather. Weather can make a huge difference in how the vehicle rides. Practice in different weather so you have a good handle on your vehicle in all situations.

Once you master driving in your RV, you may be able to bend these rules a little bit, but it is best to err on the side of caution, even after you have been driving your RV for a while.

How to Operate an RV-Specific GPS

In addition to learning how to drive your RV, you will also want to learn how to operate an RV-specific GPS before hitting the road. These GPSes are designed specifically for RV use. They provide routes that are big enough for your RV. The good news is that learning how to operate an RV-specific GPS is a lot easier than learning how to drive an RV.

If you are wondering, an RV-specific GPS is a must. Although the options below are a bit more expensive than using the built-in maps on your phone, these models will ensure you find a route that is safe for your RV. While Google Maps or Apple Maps will be able to get you from place to place in your vehicle, it does not filter options based on the size of your RV. So, splurge on RV-specific GPS systems to ensure you get to your location in one piece.

One of the easiest things to actually do is to download the RV Live GPS and Grant Campground app. It can be downloaded to your smartphone or tablet. It will use your RV's specs to determine the best route for your motorhome. It also has additional features that will make your trip planning easier. Some other RV GPS platforms to check out are the Garmin RV 785 Advanced GPS, Garmin RV 770 NA LMT-S, and the Magellan RV 9365 T-LMB. All of these platforms are designed to make it easy to find routes for your specific RV.

RV Hookups and Tanks

After you have mastered how to get around in your RV, the next thing you need to do is learn how to hook up your RV tank systems. As you know, RV hookups allow you to have water and electricity in your RV. These hookups are supplied at RV parks and many campsites. It is important that you actually know how to use water, sewer, and electric hookups to have the most enjoyable time in your RV.

The first thing to do whenever you hit a new location is to determine if they provide RV hookups and tanks. Not all RV parks and campgrounds will offer hookups. If they do not provide these amenities, you are out of luck. However, most larger campgrounds and RV parks will offer hookups and tanks.

The water hookup provides you access to fresh water for your faucet, shower, and appliances. You will need to find the RV hookup at the campground, which is typically located around the electricity pedestal. After you have parked and completely leveled your camper, connect your water pressure regulator and turn the water on. After that, hook the water up from the other end. Fill up your water tank so you have fresh water.

Campgrounds also offer sewer hookups to empty your gray water and black water tanks. This hookup is normally away from the electricity pedestal and freshwater pump. Once you locate this hookup, put on some gloves and connect your sewer hose to the pipe under your RV. Attach the other end of the hose to the sewer hookup. You will need different parts to ensure the connection is completely sealed. Feel free to leave the gray tank valve open for the entirety of your stay, but dump the black tank out whenever it is 2/3 of the way full.

With electricity hookups, you can enjoy electricity in your RV. The electricity pedestal is normally by the freshwater hookup. Plug in a surge protector and turn on the breaker. If the pedestal is not working correctly, contact campground management and wait until it is functioning. Once it is working properly, turn the breaker off and connect the surge protector to the RV's power cord. Make sure the cord is attached to your RV, and turn the breaker back on. You now have electricity in your RV.

The tips above are general and not designed for specific systems. Therefore, it is important to read the instructions for your RV, cords, and system to ensure you hook up the freshwater, sewer, and electricity hookups correctly. If you actually have any questions, you can always consult campground management for some help.

How to Winterproof Your RV

Many people do not realize this, but they must winterproof their RV before hitting the road. If you do not winterize your RV correctly, pipes can burst, and your batteries can die prematurely. For these reasons and more, it is essential to winterproof your RV every year. Whether your RV is in your garage for the winter or you are taking it out on the road, make sure to use these winterization tips:

- Insulate the RV windows. You can use foam insulation boards, solar blankets, or bubble insulation. Additionally, hang up heavyweight thermal curtains for extra warmth.

- Fill in any cracks using RV sealant or caulk. Make sure to check around the windows, doors, and vents. Fix anything that you see.

- Double check the weather stripping around your RV. Weatherstripping is normally found around the doors and windows. Replace them if need be.

- Install skirting around your RV.

- Install heat tape or insulation around your piping and existing water hoses.

- Pack extra propane in your RV during the winter, so you have enough propane to keep you warm.

During the winter, you also want to pack an additional RV kit. This kit will ensure that you and your loved ones stay safe, even in a worst-case scenario. Here are some things you should add to your RV kit in the winter:

- Heavy coats

- Warm clothes

- Heavy winter boots

- Heat tape

- Thermal curtains

- Freeze-proof heated water hose

- Rv skirt

- Ice scraper

- Extra RV antifreeze

- Mini indoor space heaters

☐ Warm blankets

Protecting the Electricals

To ensure that your RV and loved ones are protected, you must protect your electricals. Although electricals are most likely to get damaged during the winter, electrical protection is necessary year-round.

The most important step in protecting your electricals is to invest in a surge protector. A surge protector will ensure that the right amount of electricity comes in and out of the outlet. If you do not actually use a surge protector, you could hook up the electrical wiring incorrectly, which can lead to dangerous scenarios. You can even fry your electronics if you do not have a surge protector. In other words, a surge protector ensures that you, your RV, and possessions are completely safe.

There are different types of surge protection technology. The two most popular are standard surge protectors and electrical management systems. Electric management systems are the most comprehensive, which means these are the systems you should keep an eye out for. For convenience, most companies use the phrase "surge protector" in the name for these systems since most people have heard of this technology before. Here are some of the products I recommend for a safe electronic system:

☐ Southwire Surge Guard Portable 30-Amp Surge Protector

☐ Southwire Surge Guard Portable 50-Amp Surge Protector

☐ Southwire Surge Guard Wireless LCD Display

- Progressive Industries 313.1168 SSP30X Smart Surge Protector

- Surge Guard 44260 Entry Level Portable Surge Protector

- Camco 55306 50 AMP Power Defender Voltage Protector

Any one of these surge protection technologies will ensure that your RV is protected from electrical damage. Read reviews of the recommended options above to pick out the right one based on your budget and needs.

Road Assistance Coverage for RVs

Something else to think about before hitting the road is road assistance coverage. Road assistance coverage assures you that you have options if your motorhome breaks down on the road. Although this coverage is an additional price, it will come in handy in an emergency. I highly recommend investing in roadside assistance to ensure your family is safe.

When you begin looking for roadside assistance plans, read the fine print to ensure that the plan covers your RV type. Then, review other fine print details, such as the allowable towing distance and specific provisions. The last factor to consider is cost. Try to select a plan that is within your budget while still offering the maximum amount of protection.

Some of the best roadside assistance plans to check out include Coach Net, AAA Plus RV, Progressive Roadside Assistance, Escapees Roadside Assistance, Good Sam Roadside Assistance, and Family Motor Coach Association Roadside Assistance Plan. Check out all of these plans and select which one is best for your RV and needs.

RV Maintenance and Troubleshooting for Beginners

No matter how well you maintain your RV, problems will arise at one point or another. It is important that you actually know how to troubleshoot the problem so you can get back on the road as soon as possible. Here are some common problems that arise and what to do about them.

Roof Leaks

Roof leaks are inevitable for RV living. You must know how to fix a roof leak when it occurs. Try to fix the roof leak as soon as possible. Use a sealant to fix the issue. To prevent it from actually happening again, try to store your RV underneath UV resistant and waterproof cover. It is actually a great idea to invest in a high-quality cover for this reason.

Electrical Issues

Minor electrical issues happen all the time. It is important that you actually know how to do some DIY electrical repairs for minor issues. For example, you will need to learn how to use the circuit breaker. Also, look for signs that your RV batteries are dying, so you know when to replace them. For any serious electrical issue, it is best to contact a professional, so you do not injure yourself.

Plumbing

Whether you have a toilet or just a faucet, you will need to know plumbing repair tips. In addition to learning how to hook up your tank systems correctly, make sure you are only putting the right materials down your plumbing. Only select RV-safe toilet paper if you have a toilet. Do not put anything else other than human waste and RV toilet paper down the toilet. If a clog arises, know how to use a snake line. Contact a professional if you cannot remove the clog with a snake line.

If you are having leaks with your plumbing system, have a look at the pipes. See if there is any damage. If so, you may actually need to replace the pipes. You can do this yourself, but you might need to call a professional if you have no plumbing experience. Keep in mind that some RV's have specially made parts that you will have to order.

HVAC System

There is nothing worse than having an HVAC system that does not work correctly whenever you are out on the road. Always make sure that your air filters are clean. Replace them whenever needed. Keep a close eye on the thermostat as well. In RVs, it is common for thermostats to get busted. You can replace an RV AC thermostat yourself. If you need a new AC system completely, contact a professional.

RV Mechanical Parts

Like all vehicles, RVs require mechanical maintenance to stay in working order. This includes oil changes, braking fluid, antifreeze, windshield wiper fluid, etc. Learn how to make these changes yourself to save some money. If you do not feel comfortable doing these mechanical repairs on your own, know when they need to be repaired and hire a mechanic to do it for you. If something unforeseen is not working correctly with your RV, take it to the shop.

Accessories, Awnings, Etc.

There are many other features and parts of your RV you need to keep a close eye on. For example, keep a close eye on your awning or canopy. These items can get damaged quickly if you do not maintain them properly. Make sure to bring the awning down whenever the weather is harsh, and store it properly when the RV is not in use. Pay attention to other accessories, such as the detail work on the inside of your RV.

When to Call an Expert for Your RV

RVs require a lot of work and maintenance. If your RV has a foreseen maintenance or repair issue, such as leaky roof or an oil change need, you can do the job yourself. As a rule of thumb, try to inspect your RV to determine what is wrong with it from the beginning. That way, you can determine if you can fix the RV yourself. Unfortunately, not all RV repairs can be done by you. It is important to know your own limits so that you can actually take care of your RV as best as possible.

If you have no experience or confidence in maintaining your RV yourself, it is best to talk to a mechanic when any problem arises. A mechanic will help you take care of your RV as best as possible. Although it will be more expensive, you know that the work is done correctly. Even if you have some mechanic skills under your belt, there are times when you will need to contact a mechanic as well. If there is something seriously wrong with the electrical system or vehicle mechanics, it is best to contact a professional.

Chapter 20.   Safety and Security Concerns

Safety and security concerns mainly grow out of fear of the unknown. It's human nature to fear the unknown.

If there were no unknown, there would be no adventure. How much fun would that be?

Most people who are considering the RVing lifestyle have a lot of concerns, and they worry about a lot of things.

When I think about worrying, I think of the wisdom of my grandmother. She said, "Worrying must help because most of the things I worry about never happen."

Maybe she was paraphrasing Mark Twain's quote. He said, "I've had a lot of worries in my life, most of which actually never happened."

I travel as a solo RVer, and I have been doing so for more than six years. It's an interesting life. I never know what I'll encounter, who I'll meet, or how long I'll stay in one place.

I guess sometimes I know how long I'll stay because sometimes I make reservations, but that's always subject to change depending on what interesting things I find to do.

RVing is exciting, challenging, and full of amazing experiences. One of the things I particularly like about RVing is that I can change my mind and plans at any crossroad. The decisions are mine to make, and the consequences are mine to bear.

Below are what I consider to be the 11 techniques that will help you feel safe and secure as an RVer. (Note: I provided a modified version of these same 11 techniques back in Chapter 5 when discussing the topic of solo RVing. Pardon the repetition, but I think these points are important for you to keep in mind whether you're a solo RVer or traveling with someone. I also included these things in both chapters because I wanted each chapter to stand alone and completely cover the topic of the chapter.)

11 Ways to Help You Feel Safe and Secure as an RVer

☐ Arrive at your campground well before dark. Don't push it close because traffic and other factors can make your trip take longer than expected. It's hard to judge the safety of a camping place after dark, and it's a lot easier to get backed in and get set up when it's daylight.

☐ Meet your neighbors. You'll feel more like one of the family after you meet a few people. You'll also feel more secure when you know some people. It's easier to meet people before dark, so that's another good reason to arrive in the daylight.

☐ Carry Mace, pepper spray, a gun or whatever you feel comfortable with. You'll probably never need or use any of these items, but they buy you peace of mind.

☐ Have an extra set of keys in a metal magnetic box in a secure and out-of-the-way place outside your RV. Nothing makes you feel more helpless than being locked out of your RV.

☐ Have an extra credit card and a few hundred dollars of cash hidden inside your RV. There are plenty of places in an RV where you can hide things that couldn't be found if someone had all day to look for them. This could really come in handy if you lose your wallet.

☐ Have photocopies of the front and back of your driver's license and all of your credit cards, insurance cards, etc. Keep a copy in your RV and also leave a copy with an actual friend or family member.

☐ Have a GPS and know how to use it. Also, have a good set of maps.

☐ Keep your cell phone with you and keep the battery charged. You may want to keep an extra battery. If you spend much time in areas where you don't have a good cell phone signal, consider getting a cell phone booster. Also, have one of the little 12-volt to USB adapters so you can charge your phone from your RV or vehicle.

☐ Stay in one location for a week or a month or longer. When you first arrive at a place, that's when you feel the most insecure. That's because everything is unknown to you. It's natural. The longer you actually stay in a place the more comfortable you will feel there. It's simple. If you stay in each place for a month at a time, you will spend most of your time feeling comfortable. If you're moving every two or three days, you will spend most of your time feeling a little uncomfortable or apprehensive. Also, you will save money by taking advantage of the lower weekly or monthly rates, you'll cut your gas expense, and you'll have time to explore the area.

☐ Keep your RV well maintained. You don't want breakdowns while you're on the road. Replace belts and hoses as soon as they start showing signs of aging. Also, be sure to actually check the air pressure in your tires regularly. I have an automatic system that gives me a readout on the dash of the pressure and temperature of each of my six motorhome tires, plus the two dolly tires and the two back tires of my car. In addition to the digital readout, it also sounds an alarm if the pressure of any tire gets outside the safe range I've set. This gives me peace of mind. I consider this to be the best investment I've made when it comes to gadgets or modifications to my RV.

☐ The most important thing to keep in mind is to follow your instincts about safety. If you pull into a place and your gut tells you that something doesn't seem right, your house has wheels. You can leave.

☐ When you realize that security is not a problem for RVers, what else is there to worry about?

So, as Mark Twain said,

"Throw off the bowlines. Sail away from the safe harbor. Catch the trade winds in your sails. Explore. Dream. Discover."

Bottom line: Security is one of the major concerns for many people who are thinking about living the RV lifestyle, and it's a valid concern. But it's not one that should keep you from hitting the road. Just lock your doors, use common sense, and if a place doesn't look or feel safe, leave.

Chapter 21.   Suggested Arizona RV Trips

There are two wonderful RV trips to take in Arizona, depending on the sites you want to see. For a more tourist-oriented trip, you should do the Arizona North tour of the Grand Canyon and surrounding area. For a quieter trip away from it all, take the Arizona South tour through some nice small towns.

The Arizona North trip is 400.8 miles and takes about 7 hours to drive. It starts in Phoenix and circles around to Wickenburg and back to Phoenix. Phoenix is the capital city of Arizona and the perfect spot to start your journey.

While most view Phoenix as a simple stopover, you may want to take some time enjoying the outdoors here by hiking Camelback Mountain or learning about the local flora by visiting the Desert Botanical Garden. While in Phoenix, there are four wonderful activities you can do for free.

First, you can visit the Phoenix Art Museum on one of their many free days. Admission is free Wednesday evenings from 3-9pm; the first Friday from 6-10pm and the second Sunday from 12-5pm. If you visit on a Sunday, you'll even be able to take part in art-making with local artists, scavenger hunts, live performances, and free guided tours.

Phoenix Art Museum - 1625 N Central Avenue Phoenix, AZ 85004, 602-666-7104

Second, on the first Friday of every month from 6-10pm you can take part in the Art Walk. This is one of the largest self-guided art walks in the United States. There is also a free trolley. On this day, you can also get into the Heard Museum of Native Cultures and Art for free as well.

Heard Museum of Native Cultures and Art - 2301 N Central Ave, Phoenix, AZ 85004, 602-252-8840

Third, is to take a hike up Camelback Mountain. At an elevation of 2,704 feet it is a strenuous hike, but short. The mountain features two trails, both with free parking or you can take a free trolley to the trailhead.

Lastly, it is always free to visit the Arizona Capitol Museum. Here you can view artifacts from the USS Arizona that was sunk during Pearl Harbor as well as interactive exhibits about the states' role in World War II. Each day there are also guided tours available for free.

Arizona Capitol Museum - 1700 W Washington St, Phoenix, AZ 85007, 602-926-3620

Next, take about a 116 mile or about a 2-hour drive to the town of Sedona. This town is nestled among the red rocks that make the area famous. On your drive to this town, be sure to stop by the Montezuma Castle National Monument where you can hike up Cathedral Rock for stunning views of the surrounding area. On your way to the next destination, you'll come to a suggested RV park.

Montezuma Castle National Monument - 2800 Montezuma Castle Hwy, Camp Verde, AZ 86322, 928-567-3322

Suggested RV Park in Camp Verde

In the small town of Camp Verde, you'll find the Distant Drums RV Resort, it is actually just south of Sedona. It is open all year and has an average cost of $38 to $46. Pets are welcome with an enclosed dog run available. There is a total of 156 sites at this park, and it offers the following amenities:

- Internet
- Restroom and Showers
- Laundry
- RV Supplies
- Metered LP Gas
- Ice
- Cable
- Heated Pool
- Hot Tub

- Horseshoes

- Recreation Hall

- Game Room

- Pavilion

- Exercise Room

- Nature Trails

Distant Drums RV Resort - 583 W Middle Verde Rd, Camp Verde, AZ 86322, 877-577-5507

Continue your trip about 58 miles or 54 minutes into Flagstaff. Here the temperature starts to drop because of the altitude. Flagstaff is a laid-back area to stage your trip to the Grand Canyon. You can visit the beautiful Arboretum at Flagstaff or the historic Lowell Observatory where Pluto was first discovered. If visiting in the summer, you can enjoy Movies on the Square each Friday at 3 pm for free. Also between June and August, you can enjoy Concerts in the Park on Wednesdays starting at 5:30 pm for free.

Arboretum at Flagstaff - 4001 S Woody Mountain Rd, Flagstaff, AZ 86005, 928-774-1442

Lowell Observatory - 1400 W Mars Hill Rd, Flagstaff, AZ 86001, 928-774-3358

Suggested RV Park in Williams

In the small town of Williams, you'll find another recommended RV park, the Grand Canyon Railway RV Park. This park is open all year and averages $43 to

$48. This park welcomes pets and has a total of 124 RV sites. The park features the following amenities:

- ☐ Internet
- ☐ Restroom and Showers
- ☐ Laundry
- ☐ ATM
- ☐ RV Supplies
- ☐ Ice
- ☐ Groceries
- ☐ Restaurant
- ☐ Cable
- ☐ Heated Pool
- ☐ Hot Tub
- ☐ Horseshoes
- ☐ Game Room
- ☐ Playground
- ☐ Pavilion
- ☐ Exercise Room

Grand Canyon Railway RV Park - 601 W Franklin Ave, Williams, AZ 86046, 800-843-8724

Next, take the short drive of thirteen miles or sixteen minutes to Kaibab National Forest. At this park, you can hike a portion of the 800 mile Arizona Trail.

Kaibab National Forest - 800 S 6th St, Williams, AZ 86046, 928-635-8200

From here, it is an 88 mile, about an hour and a half drive, to the town of Prescott. This historic city was once the territorial capital of Arizona in 1864. As you walk through the town, you can visit Whiskey Row, which is dominated by Old West saloons.

The last leg of your trip is about 58 miles or almost an hour and a half to Wickenburg. This historic city practically oozes Wild West history. Here you can visit the Desert Caballeros Western Museum and the Vulture City ghost town with the historic Vulture Mine. You can also do a lot of hiking in the Hassayampa River Preserve. The drive back to Phoenix to complete the trip is about 66 miles or just over an hour.

The second RV trip in Arizona takes you through some of the smaller towns in the southern part of the state. The total trip is about 254 miles and takes about 4 hours. It starts in Yuma and ends in Tucson.

This trip starts in the southwestern corner of the state in Yuma. This area is popular with people seeking outdoor recreation. Since it is close to the Colorado River, you also have the option of kayaking, canoeing, and swimming. The town itself is best known for the Yuma Quartermaster Depot State Historic Park. This area is also home to some excellent RV parks.

Yuma Quartermaster Depot State Historic Park - 201 N 4th Ave, Yuma, AZ 85364, 928-783-0071

Suggested RV Parks in Yuma

In Yuma, there is the Blue Sky Ranch RV Resort. This pet-friendly resort has a total of 200 spaces and costs about $37 to $45 all year. It comes with the following amenities:

- Internet
- Restroom and Showers
- Laundry
- Heated Pool
- Hot Tub
- Recreation Hall
- Outdoor Games
- Pavilion
- Shuffleboard
- Pickle Ball
- Putting Green

Blue Sky Ranch RV Resort - 5510 E 32nd St, Yuma, AZ 85365, 928-726-0160

Another option is the Fortuna de Oro RV Resort in the foothills of Yuma. This park costs $42 to $52 all year and features an impressive nearly 1300 spaces at this pet-friendly resort. It also features the following amenities:

- Internet

- Restroom and Showers

- Laundry

- ATM

- Ice

- Worship Services

- Restaurant

- Heated Pool

- Hot Tub

- Horseshoes

- Recreation Hall

- Game Room

- Outdoor Games

- Golf Course

- Driving Range

- Pavilion

- Tennis Court

- ▢ Shuffleboard

- ▢ Exercise Room

- ▢ Frisbee Golf

- ▢ Pickle Ball

- ▢ Putting Green

Fortuna de Oro RV Resort - 13650 N Frontage Rd, Yuma, AZ 85367, 928-342-5051

A third option is the Sundance RV Resort. This park is open all year long at a rate of $37. The park is pet-friendly with 457 sites. The park comes with the following amenities:

- ▢ Restroom and Showers

- ▢ Laundry

- ▢ Ice

- ▢ Worship Services

- ▢ Cable

- ▢ Self-Service RV Wash

- ▢ Heated Pool

- ▢ Hot Tub

- ▢ Horseshoes

- ▢ Recreation Hall

- ▢ Game Room

- Shuffleboard

- Exercise Room

- Putting Green

- Pickle Ball

Sundance RV Resort - 13502 N Frontage Rd, Yuma, AZ 85367, 928-342-9333

Lastly, there is the Villa Alameda RV Resort. This park is open all year at $35. This pet-friendly resort has 302 spaces. The park has the following amenities:

- Limited Internet

- Restroom and Showers

- Laundry

- Ice

- Worship Services

- Cable

- Self-Service RV Wash

- Heated Pool

- Hot Tub

- Horseshoes

- Recreation Hall

- Game Room

- ☐ Outdoor Games

- ☐ Shuffleboard

Villa Alameda RV Resort - 3547 S Avenue 5 E, Yuma, AZ 85365, 928-344-8081

After leaving Yuma, it is a 116 mile, almost two-hour drive to the little town of Gila Bend. This town is close to the ancient Hohokam people and their enigmatic Painted Rock Petroglyph Site. East of town you can also visit the Sonoran Desert National Monument. For the hiker, there is also the Juan Bautista de Anza National Historic Trail that takes you along the path of the 1775 Spanish expedition from Nogales, Arizona to San Francisco.

Painted Rock Petroglyph Site - Rocky Point Rd, Gila Bend, AZ 85337, 623-580-5500

Sonoran Desert National Monument - W Maricopa Rd, Gila Bend, AZ 85337

The next leg of the actual trip takes you about an hour or 65 miles to get to the town of Casa Grande. Here you are placed near two very neat attractions: Picacho State Park and the Casa Grande Ruins National Monument.

Picacho Peak State Park - Exit 219 off Interstate 10, Picacho, AZ 85131, 520-466-3183

Casa Grande Ruins National Monument - 1100 W Ruins Dr, Coolidge, AZ 85128, 520-723-3172

The last leg of the actual trip takes you about an hour and 73 miles to get to Tucson. Tucson has often been an alternative to Phoenix. It serves as an excellent base to explore the natural beauty of the surrounding area.

Hiking in the nearby Saguaro National Park is a great choice, or you can visit the Kitt Peak National Observatory to learn about space. To learn about the local area, visit the Arizona-Sonora Desert Museum.

Saguaro National Park - 3693 S Old Spanish Trl, Tucson, AZ 85730, 520-733-5153

Kitt Peak National Observatory - 950 N Cherry Ave, Tucson, AZ 85719, 520-318-8600

Arizona-Sonora Desert Museum - 2021 N Kinney Rd, Tucson, AZ 85743, 520-883-2702

In addition, there are three wonderful activities in the town that you can enjoy for free.

First is the San Xavier Mission that was established in 1732. Here you can learn about Spanish colonial architecture, art, and history. You can also visit the Southern Arizona Transportation Museum for free to learn about the history of transportation in Southern Arizona. Lastly, the second Saturday of each month features free live entertainment in downtown Tucson.

San Xavier Mission - 1950 W San Xavier Rd, Tucson, AZ 85746, 520-294-2624

Southern Arizona Transportation Museum - 414 N Toole Ave, Tucson, AZ 85701, 520-623-2223

Suggested RV Park in Tucson

At the end of your trip, you can stay awhile at this resort to enjoy all Tucson has to offer. The Far Horizons RV Resort is open year-round at a rate of $35 to $55. This pet-friendly resort has 514 total spaces and offers the following amenities:

- Internet
- Restroom and Showers
- Laundry
- Ice
- Cable
- Guest Services
- Self-Service RV Wash
- Heated Pool
- Hot Tub
- Horseshoes
- Recreation Hall
- Game Room
- Outdoor Games
- Sauna

- Exercise Room

- Nature Trails

- Mini Golf

- Putting Green

- Pickle Ball

Far Horizons RV Resort - 555 N Pantano Rd, Tucson, AZ 85710, 520-296-1234

Chapter 22.   10 Common RV Mistakes

Everybody makes mistakes in life. The RV world is just like any other, with occasional mistakes that are usually made. Mistakes aren't made by newbies alone, but by experienced RV campers as well. Once in a while, they also forget to do crucial activities such as forget to carry in the RV cover or fasten the pantry well.

If you're following along in this book, then you'll have the kind of RV you want, and you'll be a pro at the terminology of the RV world. You should also have your insurance squared away, have a mail forwarding service established, and have organized your belongings to fit in the camper.

Sadly, there are mistakes about RV life that are dangerous and could cost someone a lot, including their lives. So, to be able to avoid these pitfalls that may bring about unpleasant experiences in your RV camping trip, here are a few mistakes you should avoid.

Campsite Etiquette

Many people are different and have different things they like. That is why it is actually good to be considerate of others' needs and respect their boundaries. I will discuss campsite etiquette in much more detail in a later chapter.

While at the campsite, it is a good practice to observe campsite etiquette as well as respect your neighbors. Lack of doing so may make you a bad campsite neighbor. For instance, you could be the sort of camper who makes noise for the neighbors at night, does not pick up his or her pet's waste, or carelessly empties their tanks, leaving a messy place at the campground.

All these habits will make you a bad campsite neighbor. Nobody likes living next to a bad neighbor. For this reason, it is best to observe the rules and be the best neighbor you can be in the small campground community around you. When you are considerate of others, you are likely to make new friends. Making new friends has been one of the highlights of our travels.

Not to mention that if you are a "bad" neighbor, you're probably breaking a few rules of conduct of the campground and might get evicted.

Not Bringing in the Awning

The awning is imperative when traveling with an RV as it protects one from harsh weather, provides shade, and ensures privacy in campsites that are cramped up. While it is great, this accessory is very fickle and so easy to forget on your RV.

When on your trip, you could come across high winds that could change a very good awning into a bundle of torn fabric and bent metal. For this reason, stash your awning once you detect any sign of bad weather. Everything changes, including the weather.

Don't forget the awning when you're packing up your campsite. Make sure you keep a checklist of pack up items for heading out. It's really easy to not give the awning a second thought as you're packing up to head out of a campsite.

Driving the RV Improperly

Most people assume that because they have a driver's license, they are good at driving RVs, too. Well, I have to be the one to burst your bubble, but RVs are not cars.

These vehicles are longer, taller, and weigh more than the cars you are used to. For this reason, it is essential that you consider learning how to drive one before you set out for your journey.

It's important that you learn how to properly drive your RV. When you learn, you will realize that RVs have their own techniques when it comes to things like turning, backing up, and slowing down when the winds are high.

Do not rush into driving your vehicle once you purchase the RV. Take some time and practice often before you start your trip. Most driving schools offer RV classes. In case you have a friend with an RV, you could also ask them to help you with tips and tricks on driving the RV well.

Do not assume that you can drive an RV simply because you can comfortably maneuver around with your car. Keep in mind that RVs are different!

Not Leveling the RV

I would not enjoy sleeping on an angle. Neither would I enjoy walking upward as if on a hill while inside the RV, or shower in a slanted bathroom. I bet you would not either.

For this reason, it is best to simply level the RV. Leveling an RV varies depending on the type of RV you have. However, some people overlook this process in the assumption that campgrounds are leveled. Well, this is not the case. Campgrounds, even the fancy ones, are not leveled well enough for an RV. For this reason, take the process and level your RV as required.

You should follow the manufacturer's recommendations on how to level your particular RV. There are also a number of leveling blocks and chocks on the market to assist you with leveling and stabilizing. Take the time to do this correctly, not only for your comfort but for the lifespan of your RV.

Not Disconnecting Cables

On one of our trips, my husband and I forgot to disconnect an electrical cord. We ended up driving 3 miles down the road dragging the cord behind us. It was not a good experience as others we passed were waving or honking at us, but we had no idea what the problem was.

Maybe you have seen an RV dragging a sewage hose or a cord just like we did. If you have not, do not be surprised. This is actually a common mistake that RVers make. Sometimes leaving a campground entails a lot from checking out to packing up your stuff. There is always a lot to remember. However, one of the things you should check before leaving is that all cords are disconnected and that you are not dragging any behind. Do not be like us. Disconnect your cords!

Over Packing

It is obvious that when traveling, you can be tempted to pack a lot of stuff. We women tend to think too far ahead and carry things for future possibilities.

Also, if there is enough room in the RV, why not carry everything? Well, this may sound like a good idea, but it is important to actually note that there is a weight limit to what you can carry in an RV. If you exceed this limit, your trip will not be as fun as anticipated. This is because you will have a hard time driving and stopping your vehicle. The weight can also be risky for you and other people driving around your RV.

It is good to pack luggage of a reasonable amount and not throw in all sorts of baggage, which you may not even need. To make packing easier, write down a list of the necessary things you want to pack before packing, check your list several times, and cancel out on the things that you do not find necessary for the trip. This will make it actually easier for you to carry only the necessary things.

Not Defrosting the Freezer

I know this may sound like a minor issue, but this can be quite a big deal in the life of your fridge/freezer.

When it comes to freezers, RV freezers are not similar to household freezers. In RV freezers, ice builds up over time and consumes the storage space that was there initially. This causes the freezer not to function efficiently.

For this reason, it is actually very important that you defrost the freezer. The defrosting process is very simple. You just switch the fridge off, remove the food in it, and allow the frost to melt. For faster defrosting, a hair drier or directing a fan onto the ice can be very helpful.

Forgetting to Doublecheck Everything

It is imperative that you check your RV several times before driving to any location. Before you get into the cockpit and drive, ensure that you have checked the RV properly.

Check the connection on the tow vehicle, the lights, the compartment doors outside, as well as the rig. Ensure that your satellite dish is in place, and all vents and windows are closed. Check inside the RV as well from cupboards, doors, the items stored, and everything else in the RV.

For assistance, you can use a checklist that will help you ensure everything is okay before setting off the road. Doing so could save you a lot of future problems that would otherwise occur.

Ignoring Small Problems

No matter how small the problem is, pay close attention to it and ensure that the problem is solved. This happens a lot, especially when you hit your rig on a wall or a pole, which could cause a dent and leaving a tiny hole on your rig, which creates a pathway for moisture to get into your rig, which could de-laminate your rig. Causing more problems than expected.

So, if you have something peeling off the edge of your rig, or an issue with your roof, or a leak somewhere, just stop and take care of that problem before it creates a bigger problem such as delamination, mold, and mildew, which can be avoided by just dealing with the situation.

Not Performing Proper Maintenance

Before every travel, the tires, the pressure, and the lug torque should be checked. The presence of substantial tread does not guarantee tire safety. Those tires may be ten years old and rotten to the core. Not only is it annoying if a tire blows out on the highway, but it may also seriously harm your RV.

Chapter 23.   Commonly Asked Questions

It's time to "keep it real." Even if RVing is incredible 99% of the time, it is always better to look at the good, the bad, and the ugly of the RV world before heading out on the road.

What is the worst thing about living in an RV?

☐ Being connected constantly helps you in many ways, but the challenge is to remain connected constantly. You might end up in areas where there is no internet connection or mobile service. That results in you trying to find a local café or WiFi hotspot, or worse, looking for the closest area with a connection.

☐ Be prepared for bad weather. When we are within our homes, the walls are thick so we don't worry about heavy rains or thunderstorms. When you are in an RV, however, the walls are thinner and the weather has a bigger impact.

☐ The RV maintenance. Sure, there are steps you can follow to make it easier, but it is still work and no one really likes to do that (except maintenance folks, and even they might scowl at the occasional RV-related upkeep work).

☐ Some RVs have washers and dryers while others, unfortunately, do not. If your RV is not outfitted with the aforementioned machines, you may be surprised to see just how often you find yourself looking for a laundromat.

☐ Being lonely. We have offered some advice for dealing with that, though, so make sure you use all the tips you can.

What is the best thing about RV life?

☐ You can actually live by the beach, mountains, desert, lake, or anywhere else you would like. Want to park somewhere close to the Amityville Horror mansion? You can (though in all honesty, why would you?). The freedom to travel to so many places, experiencing so many things, while living on the road is a unique feeling that cannot be described unless you have actually lived it.

☐ When you are living in an RV, you tend to spend more time outside. You are also motivated to enjoy a healthier life. Many RVers have picked up outdoor hobbies such as hiking, jogging, and rafting. You may find yourself beginning to change your life for the better.

- You cannot beat the views you see when you are traveling in an RV.

- You don't need to buy too many things when you are in an RV. You are not held down by materialistic objects; your main focus is the experience and the joy it brings. Every moment in your life is one filled with what you encounter on your journey. If the journey is as important as the destination, then being attached to your belongings is no way to experience that. However, in an RV, you are not distracted by such possessions. You are free to truly live the journey.

- Don't like your neighbors? Move.

- Don't like your surroundings? Move.

- Simply want to move? Move.

- Ever wanted to work and travel? Well, now is your chance.

- If you would like, you can stay in one place for a long time, get to know the people around you, take part in the community, and live among the locals.

- You learn to be independent, develop important life skills, and even build confidence. The RV life can influence you in many positive ways, maybe even making you become a better person.

How can you do laundry?

- You can find campgrounds or parks where there are laundromats. By using the apps I recommended earlier, you can seek more information about various sites to find if they have laundry facilities.

- Make use of the local towns or nearby cities, if you can access them.

- In many cases, people learn to do their own laundry by hand. There are many occasions where you'll have to stay somewhere overnight, which means you can wash your clothes and leave them out to dry. However, make sure you are in a safe area before doing so in case you wake up the next morning and find your favorite polo shirt missing.

- Some RVs come with washers and dryers. You can also add them to your RV, but be very mindful of the space.

Do you feel safe on the road?

- Typically, RVing is safe if you follow the rules and use a bit of common sense.

- Do not open the door in the middle of the night to people you do not recognize.

- Don't park your rig in neighborhoods littered with beer bottles and tagged with gang graffiti. That graffiti is not someone's idea of abstract expression—they are warnings.

- Don't keep your RV unlocked while you are outside. Don't keep your RV unlocked while you are inside, as well.

- Your RV probably comes with a bathroom. If you are in an unknown area, avoid public bathrooms.

- Stick to campgrounds and parks meant for RVs.

- I know it sounds nice to put up a sign outside saying, "Our home on wheels — Andy and his golden retriever, Fifi," but you are literally letting everyone know who is inside the RV. So the next time someone knocks on your door and calls your name, it may not be because they know you, but because they saw your cute sign with puppy stickers.

- Do not leave documents lying about. Keep them out of sight in a safe place.

- Crime on the road? It happens whether you are in an RV or not. If you were driving a vehicle and you felt something wrong while going down a particular path, you would immediately choose another way. Use the same sense when you are in an RV.

- I've mentioned this before, and it is worth mentioning again, keep your friends and family updated about you.

Isn't gas mileage terrible?

- This depends on how you drive your RV. I recommended earlier that you should drive your RV slowly. This is not only for safety, but for gas consumption as well.

- Another important thing to actually note is that you should turn off the electronics or appliances not in use. There are RVers who leave their television on throughout their ride and then wonder where all the gas went the next morning. Make sure you are switching off the lights, appliances, or anything else using your RV's power.

When will you start living a normal life again?

There is no specific time period for you to get adjusted to the RV life. What is important is to focus on getting used to your new home and establish a routine for the various chores and activities you might take on while traveling on the road.

Additionally, make sure you enjoy the experience. Don't think of the whole process as one big chore or requirement. Appreciate the journey and everything else that comes with it.

Can you RV full-time in the winter?

You can. Make sure you are actually aware of the local weather conditions so you prepare yourself for anything by getting the right gear.

Your RV itself can keep you warm from the elements, but the one thing you might have to be concerned about is the pile-up of snow outside. Make sure you have a shovel if you are traveling to places where the snow can accumulate.

How do you stay in shape while on the road?

The best part about being in an RV is the opportunity it brings to step outside and indulge in some outdoor activities, so don't hesitate to take a walk or go out hiking whenever you feel like it.

Do you get tired of living in a small space?

Some people do experience a sense of tiredness when it comes to actually living in an RV, but they more than make up for it by getting outdoors, being part of communities, or taking part in various activities. Just because you are in an RV does not mean you cannot head out and do something fun!

What do you do with all the poop?

As mentioned before, you dump everything into special sewer holes or dump stations. I have even provided you tips on how to keep the black tank (or the poop tank) clean.

Conclusion

RVing is an adventure. It is about the journey and the way it changes your life. But getting started on this journey can be challenging, which is why you have this book.

We have discussed how you can get started with your RV adventure. We've talked about how you can downsize your home and then pack all the essential items into your RV. We've focused on the different types of RVs you can find and what you should look for when purchasing one. Then, we looked at how you can transition to your RV life, as well as how you can travel with your kids or pets. We have gone through the waste management process and how you can perform maintenance on your RV. We looked at camping and boondocking and even found ways for you to make money while you are on the road. Solo RV was also given a special focus in the book.

With all of this information, you can get started on your RV journey with confidence. Remember to take your time with a particular step if you are feeling unsure or lost. For example, if the downsizing process is turning out to be quite a challenge, then make sure you are not stressing about it or in a hurry. Take your time and do it right. This way, you'll find yourself facing less stress in the future. Additionally, get to know your RV. Familiarize yourself with all its features and mechanisms. Take it out for a test run before you head out on your RV adventure; be comfortable with your rig and the space within. Take your time to learn about the various RV communities, which will allow you to plan your journey better. You know how to store things, what you should do if are in need of assistance, what campgrounds you should go to, and more.

But most importantly, remember to enjoy your journey.

Happy RVing.